SUMMITS
OF
SELF

THE SEVEN PEAKS OF PERSONAL GROWTH

SUMMITS OF SELF

ALAN MALLORY

PAGE TWO

This book is not intended as a substitute for the medical or psychiatric advice of physicians. The reader should regularly consult a physician in matters relating to their health and particularly with respect to any symptoms that may require diagnosis or medical attention.

Cataloguing in publication information is available from Library and Archives Canada.
ISBN 978-1-77458-091-2 (paperback)
ISBN 978-1-77458-092-9 (ebook)

Page Two
pagetwo.com

Edited by James Harbeck
Copyedited by Rachel Ironstone
Cover design by Taysia Louie and Fiona Lee
Interior design by Fiona Lee
Interior illustrations by Fiona Lee
Printed and bound in Canada by Friesens
Distributed in Canada by Raincoast Books
Distributed in the US and internationally by Macmillan

22 23 24 25 26   5 4 3 2 1

alanmallory.com

This book is dedicated to all those who want to rise above their inner challenges and limitations to take steps towards reaching new heights in life. May my journey and insights bring you hope, inspiration, and practical strategies that will empower you to incrementally improve your life and the lives of those you cherish.

CONTENTS

ACKNOWLEDGMENTS

ALTHOUGH THE writing of this book has been primarily an introspective process, there are a few people to whom I do want to convey a heartfelt thank-you for their support and encouragement throughout the journey.

Firstly, to my wife, Natalie: You have been an incredible mother to our three children, Aria, Oaklan, and Sierra, and continue to be a loving and dependable partner. My eccentric ideas and ambitious adventures aren't always the easiest to go along with, but you have been by my side throughout them all. Thank you for your steadfast support, which has enabled me to pursue a vocation I am passionate about and bring this book to fruition.

To my aunt Nancy Mallory: You are a light of hope and encouragement. I appreciate the countless times you have provided your thoughts and feedback, not only with this book but throughout the many other creative endeavors I have embarked upon.

To all the psychologists, researchers, and thought leaders whose knowledge I have incorporated throughout this book: Thank you for sharing your ideas and for your dedication towards the betterment of humanity. Your work has been invaluable in the formation of my own strategies and in the self-education and understanding that has made such a difference in my life.

Finally, I want to thank all those who have approached me and encouraged me over the years to share more of my inner journey and what I have learned along the way. Your confidence in me and sustained advocacy is what continues to make my work fulfilling and meaningful. This book is for you. Thank you.

PART I

Inner Mountains

THE INNER MOUNTAINS WE FACE

The Disaster

I remember it all too clearly. I was a young engineer, only a few years out of university, and I had been sent to a conference in St. John's, Newfoundland, to deliver a presentation promoting the engineering company I was working for. Our company was the main sponsor of the conference, and I was in attendance to represent it.

I felt a heavy burden of responsibility—to leave a good impression, but, even more importantly, to not make a fool of myself in front of my peers and the other attendees. I had experienced panic attacks and difficulty speaking in the past, and all that seemed to matter in that moment was for me to get it right so that I could avoid the embarrassment and repercussions. My career was on the line—my whole reputation, in fact—and I knew it would be devastating if I crumbled.

I was seated at one of the head tables, just in front of the raised podium, and my body was filled with awful sensations that seemed out of my control. My heart was pounding rapidly in my chest, and I felt sick to my stomach as I half listened to the opening remarks by the conference chair. I peered nervously around at the others at my table, and they stared critically back at me, clearly wondering what was wrong with me. Why did I look so sickly and agitated?

My introduction began, but I could hardly comprehend the muffled words amidst the panic I felt. I knew I would soon be called upon to take the podium and would be the laughingstock of the conference. I wanted to run and hide. I wanted to escape my impending doom. But neither of these was a viable option at that point.

As the last of my introduction was read aloud, my temperature spiked and my face turned scarlet, highlighting the beads of sweat that had accumulated on my forehead. I tried to stand, but I knocked over my chair. Everyone was watching my every move. I tried to climb the two small steps to the raised podium, but I tripped and almost fell flat on my face. My pounding heart skipped a beat at that point, and I heard a murmur pass through the crowd—as well as a few chuckles.

My surroundings were a haze but my racing mind was hyperfocused on every horrible sensation. What really terrified me was that, despite my best efforts, I felt powerless. In fact, the harder I tried to control my panic, the worse things got.

I started feeling wheezy as I stepped up to the lectern. I peered out at my executioners, who stared menacingly back. They were watching every little mistake made, and I knew what they were thinking: "What a loser! Why would the company ever send this disastrous specimen?"

I don't really remember much of what I managed to embarrassingly splutter out to the crowd before sheepishly stumbling my way back to my seat. I hung my head in devastation and barely held back my tears.

My family was ashamed of me when they found out what a fool I had made of myself. My career was ruined at that point; my future prospects were dim, to say the least. But it was my own fault that I couldn't get a grip! I had no one else to blame for my humiliating failure and the everlasting consequences.

This is a true story—except that it never actually happened. It was only true in my own mind, where I would ceaselessly rehearse disastrous outcomes in high-definition clarity. The conference was real enough, as was my participation in it, but the disastrous and unrestrained consequences were just one of the innumerable catastrophic scenarios I would tirelessly envision in the hopes of identifying and preparing for all possible threats. I was stuck in a never-ending cycle of relentlessly churning out mental movies, one after the other.

And yet I have successfully climbed to the summit of Mount Everest. How, if I am able to reach the top of the highest mountain on Earth, could I have been so daunted by an emotional mountain entirely of my own imagining?

Our Inner Mountains

We all have mountains to climb—the challenges and adversities of our lives. Sometimes we choose them, and sometimes they just appear, towering before us as seemingly impassable peaks. They are inevitable.

And that's not a bad thing. We may think we want an easy life, but much of the meaning and enrichment of our lives comes from how we work through and learn from our challenges. We define ourselves by how we climb our mountains. That's what this book is about.

We are all touched by physical, mental, and emotional distress, directly and indirectly, at many times in our lives. In fact, for many people it can seem as if life is little more than a sequence of never-ending tribulations and angst: just when one burden seems to begin to lift, we're faced with the next. To top it all off, at the end of all of this suffering, our bodies stop working and we die. We don't need to wonder why or how people become embittered with their lives and humanity in general; that is relatively easy to explain. What is not so easy to explain is how, in the midst of so much challenge and suffering, many individuals can create meaningful and fulfilling lives.

This is the heart of what we will be exploring throughout this book: rising above our hardships and perceived limitations to become the best we can. But to do this, to confront our challenges and transcend them, we must first acknowledge that they exist and begin to understand them more deeply.

Challenges are not the same thing as suffering. Our experiences in and of themselves do not axiomatically determine our emotional states. We experience things through our own conditioned lenses. Two people who experience the same tragedy often react very differently, experience different emotions, and are left feeling differently afterwards. How we react and respond to life's situations and experiences is what makes all the difference—as we'll see again and again throughout the course of this book.

On the other hand, though every mountain we face is unique, there are commonalities and pivotal ideas that can strengthen and prepare us for whatever storms life throws at us. This is the true importance of increasing our knowledge and understanding about suffering and challenges. My life isn't your life, but lessons I have learned may be useful for you.

How can I talk about suffering? I've barely suffered at all compared to many people in the world, especially from the standpoint of societal oppression and tyranny. How can anyone from a developed country with a relatively comfortable life talk about suffering? And yet we do all face suffering in our own ways. The fact of Everest's existence doesn't render Pikes Peak flat. We can always learn from how others transcend challenges even when ours appear insurmountable by comparison.

So, don't say, "That may work for some people, but they don't have the hardships I have!" I've been down that path, and I know many others who use victimhood as a defense. It serves as a justification for personal misery, and it isn't easy to relinquish such a justification, but while it excuses you from effort, it keeps you where you are, with the same hardships. This isn't to say that none of us are victims of wrongdoings—most of us can list real hurts done to us by friends, family members, politicians, strangers, and society at large—it's just that it isn't helpful or productive, especially in the long run, to hold on to these transgressions and define ourselves by them. It embitters us, and it cements our feet in place because we feel we have a reason and justification for inaction.

Of course it's tempting—and entirely natural—to compare yourself to others. But it's not realistic to look at one part of your life and compare it to one part of theirs in isolation; you don't know what else is going on with them. And when it comes to what you should do in your current situation, the important question is not whether you have it better or worse than others. No matter how dire things are or who is to blame, you need to look at where you are and how to move forward from there: what can you do and what should you do in order to make incremental improvements in your life? That is the only way onward and upward, towards the summit.

The Summits

In mountaineering, the highest mountains on each of the seven continents are known as the Seven Summits. For many mountaineers, climbing these seven peaks is a lifelong dream—and an ambitious accomplishment, considering the logistics and challenges involved.

In putting together my thoughts and research for this book, I found that many of the significant inner challenges that I and others seem to grapple with throughout life could be distilled down to seven key areas: the Seven Summits of Self.

Just as there are more than seven mountain peaks in the world, the Seven Summits of Self are not the only inner challenges that we humans struggle with. But if we focus on improvement in these seven key areas, it puts us in a very good place to work through challenges and enjoy a fulfilling life.

The Seven Summits of the world are not all equal in height and difficulty. They range from Australia's Mount Kosciuszko, which is a relatively easy day hike, through Africa's Mount Kilimanjaro, South America's Aconcagua, and Europe's Mount Elbrus, which are more significant expeditions, to the logistical challenges of Antarctica's Vinson Massif and the rigorous challenges and unpredictability of North America's Denali and Asia's Mount Everest. Similarly, the Seven Summits of Self are not all equal challenges. But unlike the literal mountains, their degree of relative challenge will vary from person to person: the Summit of Self-Knowledge might be very hard for one person and not so much so for another, while the converse may be true for the Summit of Self-Motivation. Beyond that, the chapters in this book are not all of equal length. This is in part because insights and techniques introduced in one may be referred back to by another without needing to be repeated, so each is only as long as it needs to be.

For each chapter, I have included one or more personal stories to help illustrate the importance of each internal summit and the impact it has on our lives. I then share some of the current challenges, understandings, and discoveries from science and theory. And then I bring in techniques and practical examples that I have found to be beneficial in my own journey—ones that I think you will find beneficial as well if you implement them in your own life. Each chapter ends with an "Expedition Debrief"—a chance to review, analyze, and move forward.

My first book, *The Family that Conquered Everest*, was built around my family's expedition on Mount Everest along with the experiences and adventures that prepared us to take on such a feat. It is primarily an adventure narrative, an exploration of how the frigid and desolate conditions of the Himalayas pushed us to our limits in so many ways. I found that book—the experiences that led to it, and the writing of it—easier to write than this one. Although in climbing Everest there are numerous internal challenges, the most obvious challenges are external: the volatile environment, hundreds of seemingly bottomless crevasses, oxygen deprivation, avalanches, ice slides, sicknesses, inclement weather, extreme fatigue, and a plethora of others. This book required me to dig much deeper and to ask myself a lot of tough questions along the way, many of which required significant reflection and study.

Climbing a mountain is rarely, if ever, a straight path. There are many ups and downs, twists and turns along the way. In the Valley of Silence above Everest Camp 1, for example, we had to climb down into deep crevasses, often spanning dark chasms below by balancing across ribs of ice and finally clambering our way up the near-vertical ice walls on the other side. Life is like this. We are continually faced with ups and downs. But it turns out that we need the valleys to be able to appreciate the peaks along the way. In a sense, we are ever ascending and descending as we prepare for and navigate the many peaks and valleys we find ourselves traversing throughout our lives. Some mountains we have little choice but to climb: the consequences of remaining in the valleys are beyond what we can bear, so we have to clamber our way out. Other mountains, however, are our choice to scale. There is often a deep feeling of curiosity or a self-provocation making us want to confront such challenges.

Throughout our lives we will at times experience tremendous high points where we will be filled with laughter, joy, and a sense of peace and serenity that make us feel amazing. But we'll also experience times of tremendous sorrow that make us question the justness and morality of the universe. I have been through a lot of exciting and harrowing adventures throughout my life, and this book is about my journey through yet another adventure—an adventure of the mind and spirit. Although this is a different adventure, it is no less challenging and important to confront and learn from it.

In the Forest

I was inspired to write this book by the many people who have come up to me after I've shared parts of my journey, eager to share with me their challenges and their hunger for help. They are most often desperately searching for answers for either themselves or loved ones.

At the start of my mental health journey, I thought I was a strange tree in a forest of normalcy. This added to the estrangement and embarrassment that I felt. It wasn't until after I was well on the road to recovery and had gained a decent understanding of anxiety and depression that I realized how many other people had similar experiences. But what was there to help people such as those who approach me? I found plenty of academic books and courses from psychologists and psychiatrists who specialized in mental health disorders, but there didn't seem to be much in terms of practical advice from individuals who had actually gone through similar challenges to what I was going through. When I was at the depths of my own mental health journey, I would have loved to have met someone like me who had successfully been through such a journey and who could share practical, experiential advice. People who could help the trees see the forest. That is this book.

Some years ago, my father and I had an experience with one particular tree in the forest.

It was early spring, and we decided to get our mountain bikes out for one of the first rides of the year. There is a large conservation area near the condominium where my parents were living at the time, and, over the years, various groups have established a number of walking trails and ancillary single-track routes through the hilly landscape. It is a relatively large natural forested area with challenging terrain that is great for getting out on bikes for a few hours.

As we were racing up one of the longer, gradual hills, we noticed a young man a little way off in the distance on the left side of the trail. Something looked amiss even from a distance, and as we approached him, we noticed that he had a rope strung over one of the branches of the tree; he had tied a noose at the end of the rope, and it was around his neck.

I rode off of the trail and over to where the young man was, Dad following close behind, and we dismounted our bikes quite out of breath from the climb we had just completed. The first thing I said was, "Is everything OK?"

Everything was not OK, of course. The young man—I'll call him Tim—was clearly in distress and had tears in his eyes as he looked our way.

We stayed a little way back from Tim as we talked to him. We didn't want to startle him into making any sudden decisions, since the rope was still around his neck. We were ready to swoop in if we had to, but I didn't think rushing up to him and trying to wrestle the rope away from him would have been the best thing to do.

"Are you sure you want to do that?" my father asked calmly.

Tim was a bit choked up and his voice was raspy, but he did start speaking to us. I remember saying something about it being his decision to make, but perhaps we could help him think things through more clearly. We encouraged him to share what was going on in his life that led him to this choice. As we spoke, he eventually removed the noose from around his neck and held it folded in his hand. He was frustrated and angry as he continued to share some of the details of what had been going on in his life, and in particular some distressing things that had been affecting his family lately. They were mostly financial and relationship problems that his father was going through, but Tim had really internalized these situations and the unjustness surrounding them. School and a part-time job he had were also problematic, and the whole situation of his life had become unbearable to him.

I decided to share a bit about the mental health challenges I experienced when I was in high school. He listened quietly as I shared the details about some of the distress and depression that I had faced. I shared how it is possible to get through such situations and go on to live a fulfilling life.

We asked if he had reached out for any help. He had not, as he felt embarrassed and didn't think anything could make things better. He said he hadn't really spoken about it with his father either. I suggested that he should discuss some of the things he was going through with those around him that he trusted.

We stood there and talked with Tim for most of an hour until he had calmed down and seemed to be thinking a bit more clearly. We eventually asked him what he wanted to do, and he said he wanted to walk home. We asked if we could walk with him to the edge of the forest, and he agreed. He picked up his backpack, which he had laid at the base of the tree, and we started walking, pushing our bikes beside us as we continued conversing with him.

But I was worried. Although Tim was much calmer and more rational, there was the very real risk that after we parted ways, he might just find another rope or other method to end his life. I genuinely wanted to help him as best I could, and I asked if I could email him some more information about my mental health journey that he might find helpful. He agreed, and I entered his email address into my phone.

When we got to the edge of the forest where there was a subdivision of houses, we shook hands with Tim, wished him well, and parted ways. We rode a little way up the trail and then circled back to do a quick check that he had continued home rather than turning back towards the forest. We could see him still walking down the road in the distance, so we decided to continue our ride. We weren't really sure that it was the best decision to part ways with him, but we weren't convinced that stalking him to his house or calling the police would be particularly helpful either. So we biked back to where we had found Tim, and we untied the rope, which was still hanging on the tree. It was a bit of a superficial thing to do, but it felt better than leaving it there.

As soon as I got home, I started writing my email to Tim. I wanted to get it to him as soon as possible—I didn't want him to think we weren't sincere. I decided to share some of my journey through anxiety and depression, in case it might help him. But when I started writing, I realized I had a lot more information to share than I had originally thought. By the time I was done it, it seemed more like a mini-dissertation— so long that I was worried Tim wouldn't actually read it.

I hit the send button. I was glad to see that I didn't get a bounce error; the email address was valid.

But I realized that it would be naive to think that our conversation and my email would be enough to help Tim turn his life around. My father and I discussed this, and he had come to the same conclusion. He decided to contact a friend whose wife worked in the school system with students facing mental illness and mental health challenges.

There is a protocol that the schools follow when those types of incidents are reported, which involves taking the student out of class and notifying the parents right away. We learned a few days later that Tim's father had been called to pick up Tim and take him in for a psychiatric evaluation. I wasn't sure this was the best approach, as it ran the risk of further isolating, alienating, and embarrassing Tim. If his father decided to punish him for his actions, for example, or got angry at having to take a day off work to deal with Tim's challenges, it could easily make things worse. But doing nothing wasn't a viable option—and once we had shared the information with the school system, the course was set.

I haven't been in touch with Tim much since, but he did reply to my email shortly after all of the psychiatric evaluations took place. His note was short and to the point: "Thank you very much, Alan. Thanks for contacting my school, also. Saved me a long, hard talk with my father and peers. I literally owe you my life."

It is hard to know what Tim's future holds, and there are never any guarantees that he won't relapse into a state of utter despair. I do take solace in the fact that my father and I were able to be there at the right time for Tim, and I hope the information I shared and the help that he received from medical professionals have helped him shift his life in an upward direction.

I wish I could say Tim's attempted suicide was a rare occurrence, but I can't. According to the latest Youth Risk Behavior Survey conducted by the US Centers for Disease Control and Prevention, 7.4 percent of youth aged ten to twenty-four had attempted suicide one or more times within the twelve months before the survey. Suicide is the second leading cause of death for this age group.

We have a pretty good grasp nowadays of the risk and protective factors associated with youth suicide and its prevention; we just need to do a better job as a society, particularly at the family level, of increasing protections and decreasing risks. Major risk factors include isolation, stigmatization, childhood maltreatment, hopelessness, and mental disorders. Major protective factors include family support, problem-solving skills, access to clinical care, and a sense of purpose in life.

The World Health Organization reports that one in four families has at least one member with a mental disorder, equating to around 450 million people worldwide, and nearly one million people commit suicide every year. Mental disorders are truly one of the foremost causes of ill-health and disability affecting humanity. Help and treatments are available, but the WHO has found that stigma, neglect, and discrimination deter almost two-thirds of individuals with known mental disorders from ever seeking help. It ends up being a silent affliction that slowly erodes people from the inside.

These statistics don't immediately provide a viable direction forward in terms of finding an actual solution to such challenges, but for those that are suffering, they do offer some perspective and a reminder of the simple fact that you are not alone.

Skepticism and Commitment

Many people who are searching for answers to personal problems are skeptical of advice from others. I certainly was, especially in my younger years when I was working through my toughest challenges. There were four reasons for this.

Firstly, I felt drained and exhausted, so I didn't have the energy to try anything new unless I was pretty sure it was going to make a difference. It takes time and energy to commit to new strategies, and for the most part I thought I had tried pretty much everything already.

Secondly, most of the practitioners and medical professionals I sought out had their own strategies and solutions, but in the back of my mind I always thought, "That's easy for you to say—you haven't actually been through what I'm going through!" Unfortunately, this allowed me to circumvent the essence of what I was being told and revert to my existing thinking patterns.

Thirdly, the practitioners I visited often seemed like they had their own agenda, or like they weren't really able to relate to what I was going through but had to pretend to be relatable since it was part of their job. There was also a financial incentive for them to claim to have the solutions. This may not have been fair of me to think, but it contributed to my skepticism.

Lastly, the variability in recommendations and opinions made it difficult for me to put a lot of faith in much of what I was being told and much of what I read. Where there is a great deal of variation in recommendations and ideas, it makes me question whether anyone really knows what they're talking about or whether they're just taking educated guesses. There is sometimes a degree of speculation that is passed off as expertise or certainty.

It can be natural and healthy to be skeptical. A questioning attitude helps us separate the wheat from the chaff, since we have a limited mental capacity and a finite amount of time to try out new ideas. And psychological strategies almost always take a while to implement if any real change is to be achieved, so we need to choose them thoughtfully.

On the other hand, skepticism can morph into procrastination and inaction if we're not careful. Our concern about pursuing something ineffectual or even detrimental can be an excuse to shrug off new ideas or to try them only for such a short period of time that any results become imperceptible. Major change and longer commitment are needed. It has taken each of us years, if not decades, to develop our current perceptions and ways of thinking; this isn't an easy process to go through, but we can't expect to make meaningful and lasting changes overnight.

As educator Jessie Potter said, "If you always do what you've always done, you will always get what you've always gotten." If you're not entirely happy with the many different areas of your life, you probably need a reminder of this simple but stark reality: circumstances change when we have the courage and fortitude to change ourselves. And the truth is that many, if not most, of us have some sort of mental health challenge we are working through or coping with. But it has to be your own choice and commitment to make change. No amount of external help will make a difference if it falls on unhearing or unwilling ears. This is why court-ordered psychology or psychiatric sessions usually don't make much of a difference in the lives or behaviors of the patients. If individuals aren't consciously and deliberately opening up and wanting to do the hard work of changing themselves, no amount of forced compliance will save them.

But that doesn't mean you can or should do it all by yourself. In particular, if you are suffering from something unbearable and you feel you are losing the battle, reach out for professional and practical help as soon as you possibly can. Although I wouldn't say that the counseling and advice from mental health practitioners were the cornerstone to my own recovery, they were a catalyst, and the information I gained from them was a valuable part of my journey.

What I found most valuable, though, was reading about and learning from people who had been through similar situations and came out the other side stronger and better. It takes someone who has experienced the thoughts and feelings of utter despair to fully understand what it's like—and to show the path up.

These are summits we are scaling, and there is no highway to the top. If psychology were easy, psychologists would have come to unanimous consensus years ago and moved on. They don't have all the answers, and I don't either. But I can give unique insights from my own personal experience along with my psychological and technical knowledge. When I was going through my own mental health journey, this is exactly what I was searching for. I hope it will be valuable for you in your personal journey as well. But be prepared: there is no quick fix. As with mountaineering, the journey upwards requires a dedicated, persistent, and informed approach.

So, what is the long-term solution for those struggling with internal challenges? Invest in yourself—the time, the energy, the focus, the resources, and the commitment. In today's information age, answers can almost always be found at little or no cost if you are willing to put in the time and energy. Incremental improvement is the essence of this book and the approach I've tried to take in my own life. Just like mountaineering, it is a step-by-step approach, one foot in front of the other.

Self-Worth

It can be difficult to concentrate on helping ourselves if we don't think we're worth the effort. This is a real problem! We say we want to help ourselves, and sometimes we can even convince ourselves we're being genuine, but if deep down we feel we're unworthy or underserving, we sabotage ourselves at every step along the way.

If this is the case with you, then changing your relationship with yourself should be your first priority. Self-dialogue is important in this process. Ask yourself why you feel undeserving of self-investment and what you can do to change this perception.

Are you doing or failing to do things on a regular basis that are contributing to a degradation of your self-worth?

Another common excuse, made either consciously or subconsciously, is that it feels selfish to invest in ourselves, especially when there are so many around us who are going through their own problems. Many of us, in our upbringing, have been conditioned to notice and consider the needs of others. Our sense of worth and self-respect is often tied, at least in part, to this social connection. This thought-orientation is correlated with a high level of agreeableness, a personality trait that we'll cover in more detail in later chapters. Although we may have convinced ourselves of the nobility of neglecting ourselves in favor of others, such a mentality has its detriments and is counterproductive in any practical sense.

After all, if we're going to help others, we have to be healthy and stable enough to do so. And the better we become ourselves—physically, mentally, emotionally, financially, and socially—the more empowered and effective we are in helping others. Becoming an inspiration and a teacher through your own transformation expands your possibilities for making an outside impact and strengthens your substructure so you can be a more reliable and consistent benefit to others—if you so choose.

Naturally, there are many complicated factors leading to instability and self-neglect, and I don't want to minimize or oversimplify them. The challenges and traumas are real, and sometimes almost beyond comprehension. But at the same time, there are many who have hit rock bottom who have made a personal commitment to find the answers and strength to inch themselves out of the depths of despair through conscious investment in themselves. I have had the chance to meet a few such individuals and to listen to and read about the journeys of many others.

What *do* you do if you seem to have hit rock bottom and everything seems to be stacked up against you? Start by investing in one small area of your life at a time. Make an incremental

improvement in one small area that will make a positive difference in your life. Then choose another small area where you can
invest in making your life a bit less chaotic and miserable. It isn't
easy, but there are many who have succeeded. If there is one
commonality that encapsulates all the success stories of those
who climbed their way out of the worst, this is it.

The self-improvement steps need to be small enough that you
are able and willing to take action. Be careful here. Make sure
each step is large enough to challenge you but not so ambitious
that you'll be likely to quit. Such steps may seem microscopic at
first, and that fact itself can be a barrier. It might also seem like
a waste of time, that it will take forever and never work anyways,
or you might think that you aren't worth the effort. But those
thoughts are all part of the deep chasm you're climbing out of.

Neglecting yourself can also open the door to being taken
advantage of. If you don't have plans for your development, there
are plenty of people out there who will gladly take advantage of
you to help manifest their plans for their development, at your
expense. There is joy to be found in helping other people, but
when it leads to your own personal atrophy, you will ultimately
end up exhausted, resentful, bitter, and full of regret.

It's also not so simple differentiating between a self-serving
action and a selfless action, as we'll explore in more depth later
throughout the chapter on motivation. Much of what we've
come to recognize as altruism is also beneficial to the doer,
which can make it seem like hypocrisy. But you're not doing
yourself or anyone else any favors by using that line of thought
as an excuse for inaction.

If you've been neglecting investment in yourself, now is the
time to change your mentality. You are worth the time and effort,
so make the commitment to invest in yourself today and every
day going forward.

Your Expedition Plan

In mountaineering, we almost always wear climbing packs on our backs that allow us to carry equipment for safety and survival. We usually don't end up needing all of the equipment, but it is better to have it available just in case—if you don't have the right equipment when disaster strikes, you may not survive. We need to have a similar backpack of knowledge and ideas when it comes to our psychological challenges. Every bit of information, however small, can be an important piece in the puzzle of our mental and emotional health. We might not use all of the tools and strategies right away, but we have them in our toolkit. Otherwise, we may run into trouble and have nothing to draw on.

In the end, you'll need to determine what works for you. Don't feel like you have to take advice from me, or from anyone else for that matter. I learned this the hard way. At first I was trying to do what everyone else advised me to do. But just because something had worked for someone else didn't mean it was going to work for me—as I often discovered. Eventually, I decided to live my own life. I didn't ignore advice when it was given to me, but I filtered it, acted on what I thought would help me, and disregarded the rest. You should do the same, including with any ideas I share.

You can't climb just one segment of the route, however. When we are facing a certain challenge in our lives, we often think of the challenge in isolation. We say to ourselves, "If I can just fix that one area, I'd be right as rain!" But one of the biggest personal revelations that occurs through open-minded introspection, either done individually or with the help of a psychotherapist, is that the various elements of our psyche are all interconnected.

This can be a frustrating realization. It's a bit like opening up the Pandora's box of our character. Our individual ineptitudes and areas for improvement come flooding in from all directions, and we realize we have a lot more to work on than we had originally thought. There are so many things affecting us at all times and our minds, bodies, and emotions are so interconnected that it's virtually impossible to make a change in one part of our lives without affecting others. But this also means that there are many areas that we can choose to work on and improve, and each change made will bring about changes in all areas of our lives.

Whether we like it or not, lasting change requires a broader approach involving small adjustments (and sometimes large ones) in our thinking, behavior, and other aspects of our lives. This more holistic, broader approach is what I've focused on in my own life, and I've certainly noticed the interconnections with each of the areas I've worked on and continue to work on. This holistic approach is the one I've taken throughout this book as well.

In this book, I am opening up about fairly personal aspects of my life and making myself vulnerable. I'm not naturally comfortable with doing so. I'm doing it because I know that many of you, reading this book, know exactly what the struggles and vulnerabilities feel like. I want you to know you're not alone, and I want to help you forward on your journey.

I am no longer keeping my internal struggles secret, buried deep within, and hoping nobody will find them. I became very good at doing that in my youth. I was an excellent actor, playing roles I was not feeling so I could win approval, avoid criticism, and fit in with others. Taking off that mask leaves me bare and defenseless, but I'm willing to take that risk and face the consequences, because I think it's important to be candid in order for my journey and insights to be relatable and useful to you.

Throughout the book, I share a fair bit about my internal journey, which was not a particularly happy one, although happiness is a relative emotion and shouldn't necessarily be the end goal. I am not particularly proud of the earlier parts of my journey; most of the time, I did the exact opposite of what I should have done. Often, this was due to my own ignorance—I had not learned the tools and strategies that could have prevented my downward spiral—but I also lacked a degree of courage.

So, before I serve as your guide and companion in climbing your own Summits of Self, I want to tell you about my own internal Everest—not the actual Everest that I climbed with ropes and ice axes and oxygen tanks, but the mental health journey I went through in my younger years, with its internal turmoil, storms, uncertainty, and constant setbacks. It is not a summit I would want to tackle twice, but I am thankful for one particular aspect of having made the climb: It was the reason why I started studying the human mind, and it has been an extraordinary journey.

Expedition Debrief

Your inner summits are still on the horizon, but at this point you've had a chance to survey the landscape and gain a bit of an understanding of the general route. Some foundational knowledge and background information are helpful before starting any expedition, so the first two chapters of this book are about context, commitment, and building momentum. The purpose of a debrief is to explore what worked, what didn't, and what you can incorporate in future, so now is the time to refer back to the ideas that resonated with you that you can bring forward.

What aspects of skepticism and commitment can you relate to in your own life, and how are you going to ensure that any new strategies and ideas you learn do not go unheeded? The goal is to disrupt current habits and thinking patterns by implementing practical and actionable ideas that will improve your life. In this sense, what are your beliefs around your own self-worth? Do you have any self-defeating viewpoints that you need to reevaluate? To start taking steps in the right direction, you'll need to prioritize your own self-improvement and continue building your future psychological toolkit.

Are you willing to invest the necessary time and energy to bring about internal changes? You will find that many of the ideas throughout this book build on work introduced in previous chapters, so keep an open mind and continue moving. Your summits await.

MY INTERNAL EVEREST

A Precarious Inclination

The Lhotse Face is a long, steep, icy slope in the heart of the standard route up Everest. Camp 3 is located about halfway up the Lhotse Face at an elevation of 23,600 feet (7,193 meters). If a climber thousands of feet up on the Lhotse Face dislodges a pebble, it can start a chain reaction as the rock picks up speed, dislodging larger rocks and pieces of ice, until large boulders or sheets of ice come crashing down at climbers near the bottom of the face, injuring or even killing them.

My life was changed by a chain reaction like that. But my pebble wasn't a real pebble on the real Everest. It was a moment in a high school class when I was fifteen.

Let me start with how I got to that moment.

I had an extraordinary childhood, full of experiences and adventures. I have an older brother and a younger sister, and we were all very active youth. My mother dedicated most aspects of her life to raising the three of us, and my father organized countless outdoor family adventures: white-water canoe trips, triathlons, winter camping, cross-country skiing... It was probably one of the most exciting and adventure-filled childhoods that any young person could ask for.

But I was anxious. I had a predisposition towards anxiety that was partly hereditary and probably partly learned from observing others in my extended family.

At first it only showed up before major events. For example, when I was quite young, my father got me into mountain biking and we started participating in weekly races at a local outdoors center. But each week when we were driving to the race, not only would I be almost sick with butterflies in my stomach, but I would feel sharp pains every few heartbeats as my heart pounded in my chest. My mother was naturally concerned about this, especially since my grandfather had some heart problems. She brought me in for an echocardiogram and a number of other scans and tests done by specialists, but the doctors didn't find anything abnormal.

I was also the academic of my family when I was young, and my parents set a high bar for me to encourage me to excel. If I got 95 percent on an assignment, my father would joke, "What happened to the other five percent?" He meant well, and it did inspire me to strive for perfection, but it set an expectation. I didn't want to let my parents down or disappoint my teachers, role models, and friends. I wouldn't allow myself to fail at anything. I would beat myself up through negative self-talk—and even literally: I would give myself a whack across the side of the head so I would smarten up and get things right next time.

There was something else too. When I was six years old, I was sexually abused by a babysitter who was hired a number of times to look after me and my siblings while my parents were out. It wasn't a forceful rape, but any kind of childhood molestation or statutory rape has an effect on the developing psyche. My parents were of course distraught when they learned about what had happened, and they were concerned about the long-term effects, so they enrolled me in counseling for a number of months afterwards. I remember finding the counseling sessions quite unpleasant and dreaded attending them, even at such a young age. It felt like a sort of punishment for what had happened, which seemed to augment the sense of guilt and shame I felt around the whole situation. I recall not being truthful during sessions and focusing more on the coloring and toys that they had in the counseling room while I waited for the time to expire.

But it wasn't until high school that I truly began my journey through anxiety, depression, and inner turmoil, a decade-long journey that lasted right through my university years and into my working life. I had ups and downs, depending on the situations I was in, but some of the low points were very low. And the incident that I remember most clearly, the starting point for my downward spiral, happened when I was in tenth grade.

The Butterfly and the Pebble

The tremendously complex ways that small occurrences dramatically change outcomes over time is what Edward Lorenz named the "butterfly effect," from the idea that a flap of a butterfly's wings in Brazil might, through a gradually increasing cascade of changes, lead to a tornado in Texas. And, psychologically, the way that small disruptions can morph into major challenges is one of the reasons why it is so difficult, bordering on impossible in many instances, for us to identify the specific occurrences and variables in our lives that have led to the many desirable or undesirable outcomes we are experiencing at any moment. You will never know all of the conditions that led to the effect being just as it is. But sometimes you can see something that led to something else, that led to something else . . . like a pebble dislodged from the Lhotse Face.

I was taking a tenth-grade French language class with twenty or thirty other students. The teacher was an energetic lady who was passionate about teaching and engaging students in conversational-type exercises whenever possible. A common routine for reviewing homework assignments in French class was that we would go around the room, one at a time, with each student sharing one or two responses by reading the sentences aloud to the rest of the class. It was a familiar routine to me and had never before caused a problem.

But on one particular day in class, when I was sharing one of my sentences, for whatever reason I got choked up on one of the words and couldn't seem to get the word out of my mouth for a few seconds. I'm not really sure exactly what happened—I accidentally breathed in some of my own saliva or something like that. It caused me to fumble my words and sputter a bit before I was able to finish reading.

I was immediately a bit confused as to what had happened. My heart jumped for some reason, and I did not like the feeling of not being able to get my words out. I also felt a twinge of mild embarrassment at having gotten choked up like that in front of my peers.

Shortly after that, the class was dismissed, and I went about the remainder of my day as I did any other day at high school, with nothing other than a strange bewilderment and uneasiness about what had happened and why.

The following day was fine as well, until I took my seat in the French class. Then I remembered the choking incident and started thinking more about it as I waited for class to begin. One of the first things we did was start the routine of going around the classroom with each student sharing one or two responses. I was in approximately the middle of the classroom, and as the other students began sharing their responses one by one, I felt an uneasiness grow inside of me and began picturing myself getting choked up on my words again, as I had done the day before. It was a slow process that particular day as the teacher continued calling on each student in order, row by row, slowly approaching where I was sitting.

By the time it was my turn, I was so fixated on my own internal feelings and bewilderment about why and how such feelings were happening within me that I again got choked up on my words. And I felt embarrassed again, even more so than I had the previous day.

Since I was once again feeling humiliation, I started thinking more and more about why this was happening. The more I thought about it, the more anxiety welled up inside me about the possibility of having to go through that situation again. I started to relive the situation in my mind over and over again, still wondering why and how it had happened.

Eventually, it consumed my thoughts, and I started envisioning myself getting choked up and not being able to speak not only in French class but in other classes and other social situations. I was afraid of making a fool of myself and being laughed at or looked down upon by the rest of the class.

I started avoiding situations where I knew I would have to speak in front of groups of people and eventually even avoiding situations where I envisioned the *possibility* of having to speak in front of other people. Avoidance seemed to me at the time to be the best way to ensure I didn't experience further perceived failures. I continuously ran all hypothetical situations through my mind to try to see if there was a chance that I would be asked to speak, and I found that probability almost everywhere. I became very good at circumventing such situations. I would ask to go to the restroom, for example, and would sit in one of the stalls, my heart racing with anxiety, for long periods of time until I thought the "danger" had passed, at which point I would timidly return.

The Boulder

The anxiety got worse and worse and started to affect many other areas of my life. I was fearful of talking to anyone I viewed as an authority figure, for example, and I would avoid these situations whenever I could. It did seem to matter who initiated the engagement: if I was the one who approached the authority figure, I felt in control and had very little anxiety. But when I was asked to meet with the school principal or given a specific time when I was scheduled to speak with a teacher, my anxiety would mount.

I had gradually developed a full-spectrum social phobia that was affecting a broad range of daily encounters in my life. I would choose my courses, for example, based on which ones I thought were least likely to have presentation components or incorporate large group discussions. At one point, I ended up dropping a biology course within the first week when I found out about the presentation requirements throughout.

At times, I wasn't able to avoid social situations, no matter how hard I tried: a post-secondary planning meeting with the school guidance counselor and a small group of other students, or a compulsory class presentation. For the days or weeks preceding these events, I would worry continuously, envisioning all the negative outcomes that could possibly come to pass. I would picture myself unable to speak or my face turning red in front of my peers. I also frequently envisioned fainting, which didn't seem that much of a stretch, since my anxiety would cause me to get dizzy or lightheaded at times. When my turn for a presentation arrived, I would have worked myself up to the point where I could hardly function: my heart was racing, my face was red, I couldn't control my muscles properly, I trembled as I walked to the front of the class, and I could hardly get the shaky words out as I bumbled through them as fast I could before shakily sitting back down, embarrassed, exhausted, and feeling utterly humiliated.

Interestingly enough, the times when I was most relaxed and comfortable were when I had exhausted myself to the point that I could no longer remain vigilant. I would wearily let my guard down, almost from necessity in that I had exhausted so much of my energy or cognitive ability that I gave up. It was physically, mentally, and emotionally draining to be continuously on alert for emotional triggers and potential situations that I had flagged as socially dangerous, but I didn't seem able to consciously let down my guard.

There seemed to be no end to the awful physiological sensations and experiences that accompanied my anxiety—profuse
sweating, hot flashes, difficult breathing, trembling limbs, racing
heart rate, chest tightness, twitching muscles, nausea, and an
overall feeling of numbness, to name a few—and these sensations
were especially heightened during my frequent panic attacks.
Our bodies are very creative in the varied symptoms associated
with panic, and I got to experience the whole spectrum.

Other than the few friends that I had from my elementary
school that attended my high school, I became more or less a
loner, especially in my first couple of years of high school. I took
the bus almost every day to and from school but would generally sit silently in my seat, barely uttering a word. One semester,
I spent the vast majority of my lunch periods wandering the
streets of downtown Barrie, Ontario, where the high school was
located, counting down the minutes until the next class was set
to begin. My internal dialogue was going at full speed, but I was
a quiet and reserved kid on the outside. I thought it was better
to remain silent than risk embarrassment.

For my latter years of high school, I moved to a new school
where I had a few more of my friends from elementary. What
was interesting was that when I was among my smaller friend
groups or family circles, I was like a whole different person. In
the absence of my anxiety, I was an outgoing and talkative kid, so
few people, if any, would have guessed that I was suffering from
a social phobia. My move to the new school was an improvement
in terms of my social life—but my fear of group humiliation and
the related anticipatory anxiety didn't improve.

I discovered alcohol in those years, and I soon realized how
it numbed my feelings and dampened my concern for future
consequences. Under the influence of alcohol, I could party in
any sized group and rarely felt embarrassed or anxious. There
were plenty of nights where I would join my neighbor, who was
around my age and had plenty of challenges of his own, and we
would find one of his grandmother's bottles of rum or vodka

and pour a good portion of it out for us before filling it back up with water to the same level. She didn't seem to notice most of the time, until it was really watered down. There were also a few times we drove into town and convinced one of the homeless people hanging out by the liquor store to buy us a bottle of rum or whiskey in exchange for a few bucks. Eventually, I got my hands on an old driver's license from my older brother, Adam. Since we looked quite similar, I had a fake ID at my disposal. On the weekends, I would often go to country-music dances where I would drink and party with friends, often spending the night in a truck camper in the parking lot afterwards. I felt like a cool kid again, and careless partying was a lot of fun.

But it wasn't a good idea, and I almost lost my life more than once. One time, after we had been drinking and dancing in a club in Toronto, my friend who was driving fell asleep behind the wheel and crashed his pickup into a steel traffic light while I was asleep in the middle of the front bench seat. Luckily, the truck sheared the steel pole off, which minimized the impact. Another time, we were driving down an active railway track in a friend's truck and got stuck broadside trying to turn around. It was only our good luck that a train didn't come by in the time it took us to push and maneuver the truck free.

And after all that, after the fun and the danger, after the hang-overs and headaches subsided, I would be back to my anxious sober state and dreading my reality.

The Crash and Fall

When I went to university, I chose to study engineering, in part because I didn't think it would have many presentations or as much social interaction associated with it. I chose my electives with an eye to avoiding speaking and social embarrassment as well. But I had bouts of anxiety and panic almost every day, usually just from situations I envisioned that never did actually come to pass.

My frequent panic attacks led me to be always on edge, watching for social situations where I might be publicly humiliated. I started trying to self-diagnose and self-monitor, so I was always focused on the uncomfortable feelings that I had inside. I couldn't fully understand why this was happening to me. It seemed so automatic and impossible for me to influence in any helpful manner. I was lost inside my own mind, and the things going on around me were increasingly hazy—except when I was having a full-out panic attack from a social situation, in which case I would be hyperaware of everything that was happening around me and keeping an eye on every minute detail.

This developed into what psychologists call generalized anxiety disorder (GAD), a persistent and ever-present state of worry and anxiety. I was experiencing anxiety almost all the time in those days. My anxious state had become my new baseline, fluctuating from minimally anxious on good days to horribly anxious on bad days. Eventually, I didn't even need a visual trigger at all in my mind. The feelings of anxiety themselves were what caused more anxiety, and this cycle continued day after day. It was truly a self-fulfilling prophecy; my symptoms themselves perpetuated the ever-present stream of additional symptoms.

I hated the anxious feeling inside me, and I hated that part of me. I was angry at myself for letting such a thing happen in the first place, and I continuously blamed and belittled myself for everything bad that was happening in my life. I thought that I needed to find the solution to my problems by thinking my way out of what I had gotten myself into. I would relentlessly try new ways of analyzing and discerning what was happening to me and new ways of trying to influence the outcomes. Even though nothing seemed to work, I just tried harder. I was testing all kinds of different techniques and frantically searching the internet for new ideas each day for the "magic fix" to my inner turmoil.

The anxiety was no longer associated just with speaking and social situations. It affected my relationships, my ability to sleep, my irritability, my concentration, my decision-making, my leisure time, my ability to take advantage of opportunities... I was terrified that one or more of my peers, friends, or family members would discover my problems, which I viewed as extreme weakness, so I learned to present myself on the outside as a confident person, hiding the reality of my inner turmoil. I became a good actor, you might say, and adopted the persona of a calm, cool, and collected individual. So most of my family and friends hadn't the faintest idea what was going on in my life—and I wasn't about to let them in on it for fear of having them look down on me.

It's hard to say exactly when my high levels of anxiety morphed into depression, but at one point I just started losing hope that I would ever recover, and the sadness associated with that perceived reality sank my spirits to a whole new low. I felt, almost continuously, a deep sense of sadness and hopelessness. Things that would normally cause me joy did not, or at least not nearly to the same degree. They were replaced with a dull sentiment of self-pity, a constant feeling of being sorry for myself and the dismal internal life I was struggling through.

Because I felt so hopeless and confused inside my mind, I started viewing most experiences through a more negative lens, one that often didn't reflect their actual valence. I would focus fully on the negative aspects of the things that happened to me and the situations I went through, to the point where I perceived the majority of my outcomes as being yet another series of failures. This just increased my depressive thoughts and led to more horrible mental and physical sensations, and the cycle continued. I saw my life as a series of internal problems, and I would even internalize other people's problems. I would endlessly ruminate on bits of negative news.

For a period of time, I was experiencing awful heart palpitations. From these, in turn, I lost sleep; I would lie awake, observing and anticipating the irregularities in my heartbeat for much of the night, and I would often wonder if my heart might stop altogether during one of the missed beats. I was disturbed about these palpitations, so I went to see a doctor, and he put me on a heart monitor. It had electrical leads connected to areas of my chest, and I wore it twenty-four hours a day for a week to record my heart function. I had to press a button on the device to log when I would feel an irregularity, which was most often as I was trying to go to sleep. And in the end, the doctor concluded that there weren't any physical abnormalities with my heart.

I started seeing various doctors, counselors, psychologists, and psychiatrists. Some told me that underlying my anxiety and depression was a hereditary predisposition to a chemical imbalance. I was given books to read, printout materials, and many suggested medications. I was concerned that I would become reliant on medication and it would mask my symptoms without addressing the deeper cognitive causes, so I chose not to medicate, knowing it could be an option if needed.

And yet my life was still moving forward through all of this. I got my degree, I got a job as an engineer for an international firm, I had a social life. I got married in the summer of 2010. My wife, Natalie, was quite supportive but didn't really know what she could particularly do to help.

One week after our honeymoon, we packed our bags and relocated to Santiago, Chile, to work for a few years out of one of the engineering firm's satellite offices. To try to clear my head, I would often wander through the park near our apartment or down random streets feeling immensely sorry for myself, hopeless in terms of any sort of recovery, and unable to turn off my depressive thoughts or rid myself of the terrible inner feelings.

One of my worst depressive episodes happened when I was sent to the engineering firm's Calgary, Alberta, office for a few days to take part in a project management training program. The experience during the training program itself wasn't too bad, although I was on high alert throughout the entirety of it for the possibility of being singled out, and I had no shortage of anxiety around the group discussions. But in the evenings, I was all by myself with nothing to do other than ruminate on my own feelings, and the unpleasant sensations in my chest and the pit of my stomach seemed especially terrible. I wanted to escape the feelings and rid myself of that part of me. I decided to go walking to try to distract myself.

In the downtown core of Calgary, because of the bitter winters and wind, the city has coordinated the building of enclosed walking bridges that connect the majority of the office buildings and hotels. There are now more than eleven miles of corridors in this network, so I had plenty of space to wander. The corridors and buildings were mostly deserted at the time of night I meandered through one after another, trying to figure out my depression. My mind raced as I frantically tried to control or diminish the terrible feelings inside me. I couldn't get my mind off of them, no matter how hard I tried. I remember biting my lower lip angrily in an attempt to punish myself for my failure to snap out of my depression.

Being relentlessly tormented by your own mind is a terribly cruel and debilitating situation to be in. There is little wonder why people want to escape such self-torture at any cost and often resort to drastic measures.

What Had Happened

Before I come to how I moved up and out from that place, I want to unpack what had happened to me, now that I understand it better from a psychological perspective many years later.

The initial trigger event of getting choked up and being unable to speak was a relatively minor occurrence that I could have brushed off as such. However, it frightened me, and when I was faced with a similar situation the following day, it triggered a stress response in me that is often referred to as *fight-or-flight*.

This physiological response is a survival mechanism whereby a sudden release of hormones activates our body's sympathetic nervous system. Our adrenal glands then trigger the release of adrenaline and noradrenaline, which increases our heartbeat, redirects blood to our muscles and brain, dilates our pupils for better vision, and tenses our muscles for rapid action. We are primed to either fight the threat or flee. The fight-or-flight stress response has tremendous utility for when we are faced with real threats, but it can also be triggered by perceived or imagined threats, as is the case in almost all psychological disorders.

When I was in high school, I didn't know anything about this acute stress response or the long-term implications of fleeing from such perceived threats, so I fled every time I was faced with a situation that could result in social embarrassment. I then adopted avoidance mechanisms to avoid similar perceived threats in future, which strengthened my own convictions in these threat beliefs.

The disaster thinking and continuous envisioning of failure scenarios also served to bolster my ill-conceived beliefs around the dangers associated with public scrutiny and related public embarrassment. Social humiliation is one of our basic fears as humans, and I had made the connection that being in the spotlight in social situations would inevitably lead to such humiliation.

The fact that I would routinely run away from social situations, and that my fear response would subside temporarily whenever I did flee, was all the proof my mind needed that the situations were dangerous. Isolated incidents would be bad enough, but the frequency with which I replayed and pre-played incidents in my mind led to a concrete conviction about such fear.

Our minds can't distinguish very well, in terms of our subconscious emotional learning, between situations we go through in reality and scenarios we play out in our mind's eye. As it happens, I have somewhat of an eidetic memory, which has been quite helpful throughout my life but is also related to how vividly I can imagine future scenarios. The result was that the scenarios and disastrous consequences I constantly played out in my mind not only seemed real but were accompanied by the same emotional responses, so I subconsciously justified and strengthened these irrational fears.

There is practical utility in our ability as humans to abstract and project in order to envision ourselves in future scenarios. This is what is known as *episodic future thinking*. It allows us to avoid in reality a path on which we get hurt or fail in our minds. The problem is that episodic future thinking can be taken too far, which is what unwarranted rumination about future events really is. There is no limit to the number of future scenarios we can envision, and it can easily become an obsession, especially when fear is the driving force. Our minds are creative and can almost always envision many different dreadful scenarios, ones we wish to avoid allowing to come to pass. Thus, we can become endlessly fixated on discovering all such scenarios for preparation and avoidance purposes. The thought projection that I shared at the very beginning of this book is an example of episodic future thinking.

That was phase one of my decline: envisioning countless scenarios of perceived threats, experiencing the associated anxiety, and retreating to avoid all such scenarios.

The next phase of my spiraled decline began when I created a positive feedback loop in my psyche. A *positive feedback loop* is similar to what you get when you hold a microphone too close to a loudspeaker: The initial sound into the microphone is amplified through the loudspeaker; because the microphone is so close to the speaker, it picks up that sound and sends it back to the speaker, which plays it back amplified, the microphone picks it up, and the re-amplification continues. This process happens quite quickly, and the system overloads, producing a deafening screeching or squealing noise. Modern sound systems have controls in place to limit the maximum amplification; without them, the signal will increase indefinitely until the speakers—and perhaps your eardrums—are blown.

I experienced something similar psychologically, and it's the same effect that occurs with most psychological disorders and phobias. Eventually, I didn't even need a perceived external threat or the envisioning of such a threat for my anxiety response

to be triggered. All it took was the conscious noticing and reacting to my present state of anxiety to fuel the additional anxiety.

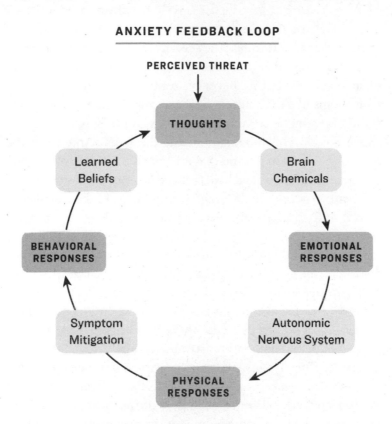

ANXIETY FEEDBACK LOOP

PERCEIVED THREAT

THOUGHTS

Learned
Beliefs

Brain
Chemicals

BEHAVIORAL
RESPONSES

EMOTIONAL
RESPONSES

Symptom
Mitigation

Autonomic
Nervous System

PHYSICAL
RESPONSES

It became a self-fulfilling prophecy. The more I noticed anxiety within me, the more anxiety I felt, and the positive feedback
loop spiraled out of control. My only escape from this continuous
loop of increasing anxiety was when I was significantly distracted
by external stimuli that would pull my attention away from my
inner feelings of anxiety, or when I became so exhausted that my
mind would more or less just shut down. Ironically, when these
states of utter exhaustion would overtake me, I finally felt free
of the anxiety for short periods—until I had the energy again
to continue the self-diagnosis, self-criticism, and self-sabotage

cycles all over again. It was like unplugging the microphone. But I would always plug it back in again.

What I have just described is GAD. Once the positive feedback loop has been established, the sufferer lives in a constant state of anxiety and inner turmoil. The severity may increase or decrease based on external and internal factors as well as chemical and biological ones, but it is ever-present in one form or another.

It seems like the solution to these types of mental disorders should be simple. All the sufferer has to do is switch off the feedback loop and stop re-amplifying the signal. And that is the solution—but I can tell you that it is much easier said than done. The thought patterns and beliefs at the heart of the disorder have had years to develop and strengthen, and most of them arise very quickly and primarily take place automatically at an unconscious level—buried so deep as to be almost inaccessible. It's become a *reflex* to plug the microphone back in. Unlearning that reflex doesn't happen overnight by any stretch of the imagination.

The terms *subconscious* and *unconscious* are often used synonymously, but the distinction is important when it comes to our ability to observe and influence thought processes. Austrian neurologist Sigmund Freud was instrumental in much of our current understanding of consciousness, dividing human consciousness into three levels: conscious, subconscious (or *preconscious* as Freud put it), and unconscious. Our *conscious* refers to the thoughts, memories, feelings, and senses that are currently in our focal awareness, whereas our subconscious consists of processes that are not currently in focal awareness but can be brought into awareness through introspection and our unconscious contains all experiences, feelings, urges, and other mental processes that have been repressed, are no longer accessible, and occur automatically. What makes psychological disorders such as that which I experienced so complex is that, while some problematic mental processes can be accessed and analyzed at the subconscious level, many stem from deep recesses at the unconscious level and are no longer accessible through introspection—altering unconscious processes is much more difficult.

Recovery

In the end, I was more fortunate than some others who get stuck in the feedback loop indefinitely. I had the access to information, the time, the cognitive ability, and the persistence to do something about my situation. Perhaps I stumbled upon the right books at the right time, or perhaps I was just stubborn enough to refuse to give up. I think this stubbornness, which also had an element of persistence and resilience fused with it, was an important factor in my recovery. It also took a lot of courage to face internal challenges, and I am proud of myself for being willing and able to take the necessary steps.

I say this because if you are embarking on a similar journey, I commend you for your own resolution and I want to encourage you to persevere. You may still feel like you are frozen at the base of your mountain and are being knocked back down with every step you attempt, but even the wrong steps tell you something: what paths to avoid. You will find a foothold eventually, and in the meantime, you can feel good about your own courage and determination.

I'm not sure exactly when and why I made the decision to start taking a deep dive into psychology. I had a career in engineering! But I recall that at a certain point, years into the disorder, I decided that enough was enough. Rather than continuing along the path that I had been on for many years, I was going to devote my energy into self-education and figuring out what was at the root of my anxiety and depression. I also decided that I was willing to go through whatever frightening or uncomfortable situations presented themselves along the way, and I wasn't going to let anyone or anything get in the way of my doing so.

As you know by now, I had expended huge amounts of energy before in thinking about my inner problems and playing things over and over again in my mind. This time, however, I took a different approach. I started studying how the human mind works, from the basics of the fight-or-flight response and how it evolved, to more advanced areas of how our brains regulate chemical levels and the behavior and characteristics of our subconscious mind. I discovered that there were many books written about anxiety disorders and social phobia, and I decided to start reading them. I had already read the basics from some of the material that the medical professionals had given me over the years, so I had a rudimentary foundation, but most of what I had read was theoretical rather than practical.

I ended up learning a bit about all kinds of unique practices, from meditation to hypnosis, and I began using the techniques that I learned along the journey. I read a fair bit about mindfulness and relaxation techniques in particular. Many of the concepts and books I read seemed foreign to me, especially the concepts around bodily energy and the interconnected forces between all things in the universe. I decided to absorb it all with an open mind and not write anything off until I had given it a fair evaluation. After all, my beliefs and thought patterns up until that point hadn't exactly left me in a good place, so who was I to judge?

I also took other steps in addition to reading. I joined a Toastmasters club, which was a safe environment for learning and practicing public speaking, for example. At first I was terrified to attend the meetings, but I pushed myself to do it anyways. I convinced myself to volunteer for and go through many of the other social situations that I was terrified of. Instead of going through them because I had to, with the mentality that I just wanted to survive, I was approaching them voluntarily with an exploration mentality, trying to learn from what happened and make incremental improvements each time.

Though I didn't know it then, that makes a big difference. Being forced to go through situations has little positive effect and can actually exacerbate the problems, but facing your fears voluntarily activates a different circuit in your brain and allows the positive improvements to take form incrementally. Every time I would get through one of these social vulnerabilities, I would feel a tiny sense of accomplishment and self-satisfaction inside. I had faced my fear and survived—and survival was an internal victory! The interesting thing was that the next time I had an occasion to put myself out there, it was ever so slightly easier to volunteer, and I felt ever so slightly less anxious in doing so.

One of the most important things was that I continued experimenting and practicing with many of the things I learned. When I would start to beat myself up over something I thought I had done wrong, I would stop myself, take a deep breath, and say to myself, "This is OK that I've screwed up, I'll get it right next time or the time after that." Then I would move on. I practiced accepting setbacks as learning experiences. When my mind would start racing and playing mental movies of past or future negative events, I would consciously stop my mind from going down that path and focus on a positive, or at least helpful, element instead. Or I would rewrite the ending of the movie and picture myself as a confident person and with a successful outcome, even when such an outcome seemed awkward or unlikely. And I continued studying mindfulness and different ways of calming my mind and body. In a situation that I would normally stew over for days or weeks, such as being yelled at by an authority figure or getting turned down by someone, I would think about how I was still OK and would focus on positive response strategies that would move me forward. By changing the way I reacted, I was able to notice opportunities within the challenges I faced, and some things that I originally labeled as disaster ended up being some of the best things that could have happened to me.

And yet, with all of this, very little of my external situation had changed. I still had many of the same challenges and concerns that most people have—around money, employment, education, friends, health, extended family, etcetera. But these things did not seem to be nearly as much a burden on me anymore.

One thing that did change was my career. I eventually went on to get a master's degree in psychology from Adler University. And I don't plan on stopping learning anytime soon—so, who knows what the future will bring. But the first thing it will bring is the rest of this book.

Reflection

The old adage "they'll grow out of it" is foolish and careless. It is possible for people to solve psychological problems simply by mere chance and circumstance, but it's very unlikely. More likely, if you ignore problems and hope they'll work themselves out, they'll just get worse. Even if it seems like things couldn't get worse, that you've finally hit rock bottom, you will find that there's even farther down you can go if you keep digging—doing what got you there in the first place.

And those who tout the "grow out of it" or "snap out of it" mentality senselessly underestimate or completely miss the reality of what the natural progression can be when left unchecked. Entropy applies to everything in the universe, including the human mind, and miraculous improvement isn't the norm. You can't tell someone at the bottom of a deep crevasse to just step back up to where they fell from.

On the other hand, you don't have to stay at the bottom: I'm a firm believer in adopting a transient mentality when it comes to mental health disorders. Yes, there are long-lasting and even permanent chemical and biological factors that contribute to mental disorders, but we must not let them be a self-fulfilling prophecy. I have seen how a diagnosis can deflate people and lead them to accept the corresponding limitations. A disorder is not you, it should not define you, and you have the ability to improve. Your brain can adapt, reorganize, and undergo physiological changes in response to experience, from the day you are born until the day you die. This is known as neuroplasticity. Even stroke victims and paralysis patients have been able to regain bodily function through their brains' rewiring and creating new neural connections.

But as you work on coming out of a mental health crevasse, be careful about the difference between digging your way out and just digging in further. For most things in life, a curious and analytical mind is a good thing: it lets you run different potential solutions through your mind until you can come up with a working way forward. But with mental illness, and particularly GAD, a continual focus on and analysis of the symptoms can perpetuate the disorder.

This self-sabotage was something that really took me a long time to get my head around. I thought I could make the terrible feelings go away by thinking about them in clever ways and continually trying to fight against what I was experiencing. At the very least, I thought that I could consciously and directly influence my condition through sufficient analysis and infusing the right thoughts at the right time into the chaos that I felt. But in the end, it was the continual self-evaluation and the acute focus on my problems that kept me stuck in the never-ending cycle of anxiety. It was a self-fulfilling prophesy by its very nature, and I was sabotaging my own life with it. The analysis brought with it bewilderment and frustration as to why I couldn't defeat my anxiety despite my best efforts, and it kept me focused on my problems.

So what is a person to do? Look up, not down. There is value in working to find the causes of your psychological challenges so that they can be properly addressed and ideally transformed, but it must not become an obsession. Learn from the past for self-healing and self-education, to create a brighter future for yourself and those around you. Nothing good will come from blame, victimization, and holding onto old grudges. Life happens in the present—don't miss out on it.

How We React

I've met a number of top business executives and have been bewildered at first by how they could be so miserable. They had almost unlimited money, a huge amount of influence, and could seemingly buy or negotiate their way out of any problem that faced them. But they could not buy happiness or fulfillment, and they were miserable inside. If those in the upper echelon are in such dire straits, what hope does that leave for the rest of us?

I've also had the chance to travel to a few of the poorest places in the world, where millions of people don't have electricity or a place to live and many aren't sure where their next meal will come from. And yet I saw laughter, family bonding, and happiness. At first I thought, "How could this be? These people have almost nothing and are faced with more challenges to deal with than I could ever imagine. What could they possibly be joyful about?"

Eventually, I put it all together. I had experienced both mentalities myself. In my depression, I would react with despair to everything that happened to me, focus on everything I didn't have, and be consumed with the negative situations and feelings I was faced with. When I began to recover, I would react to the exact same situations with acceptance, hope, and a focus on what I did have and the positive elements of what I was going through. My external situation was more or less the same in both instances, but my reactions and internal thought patterns had changed. Instead of sadness, depression, and despair, I was filled with a degree of internal peace, acceptance of what is, and excitement about the future.

It's not that I stopped feeling bad. We all feel bad sometimes. I stopped feeling bad *about feeling bad*. I started observing myself for who I am and the situations around me for what they are. I started fighting less and accepting more, particularly those aspects that I couldn't change or was currently unwilling to change.

It is a bit hard to explain, but during the low period of my life I was treating that ball of anxiety in the pit of my stomach as something foreign that I needed to rid myself of. I kept trying to fight it and drive it out of me. When I was ultimately free of it was when I finally decided to stop fighting and accept that part of me, even love it on a deeper level. I say deeper level because I had already tried accepting it at earlier times, but I didn't *really* accept it, I just wanted to trick myself into believing I did: I was saying the words inside my head while still hating that ball of anxiety. It didn't work until I was finally, after years of learning about myself, able to get to it at a deeper level of self-acceptance and love. Then it melted away.

This isn't to say that I now ignore my shortcomings. There is a balance between self-acceptance and self-discipline that we'll explore in more detail later.

For me, my path to recovery from depression took me on an extraordinary journey. With the volunteer speaking engagements I was doing, ironically I began to start to enjoy public speaking. That which I feared most became a true passion of mine, and now I travel all over the world delivering presentations and workshops to groups of sometimes over a thousand people at a time. I found my deeper passion, decided to pursue it, and am so happy that I did.

Expedition Debrief

I have shared the ups and downs of my own journey, but this book is ultimately about you, so be honest with yourself about your internal experiences and where are you starting from. Are you prepared to tackle the summits outlined in the coming chapters? My objective in sharing my journey is for you to think about your own psychological ups and downs and how you may be able to learn from my experience to strengthen yourself and avoid future pitfalls. You'll be encouraged to think deeply and reflect upon your own past events at various times throughout this book. Use these reflections only in helpful ways that will brighten your present and future reality.

Be wary of fighting yourself and your inner reality along the way. Even the aspects of yourself that you do not like are currently part of you, and you have to start by accepting where you currently are. The constant battle is futile when you are both the perpetrator and the victim—put down your weapons and bring yourself together so you can move forward in a holistic fashion.

Have you adopted some of your own avoidance mechanisms? What are the situations you tend to avoid? These are important to identify, as we'll be referring back to them. Remember that, from an experiential perspective, your reactions to circumstances are critical, often more important than the circumstances themselves.

You now have the background information and context around the areas of self-improvement we'll be exploring. You are standing in the foothills gazing up at the mountains ahead of you. Strap your crampons on your mountaineering boots and grab your ice axe. It's time to start climbing.

PART II

The
Summits

THE SUMMIT OF SELF-KNOWLEDGE

Denali

It was late in the day, and my father and I were exhausted. We swung our heavy packs off our backs and rested for a few moments before beginning to set up our tent. We had just arrived at High Camp, 17,200 feet (5,242 meters) above sea level on Denali, the highest mountain in North America. I was nineteen years old, and it was my first major mountaineering expedition.

We had been climbing for nearly two weeks already, and that day we had climbed nearly three thousand vertical feet and navigated the narrow ridge where the famous Washburn's Thumb boulder is situated. We were in Alaska and it was summer, so we had twenty-four hours of daylight.

I had gotten temporary snow blindness at lower altitude. I had also injured both of my Achilles tendons trying to pull one of our gear sleighs that had flipped over and was stuck near the edge of a giant fissure in the ice. The Kahiltna Glacier, which we had been following for many days, had been particularly unnerving because of the deep hidden crevasses it is famous for. The intense wind blows snow over them, creating snow bridges that hide them but can give way as you step on them, releasing you into the dark depths below.

Our arrival at High Camp was an important milestone, and I was looking forward to a much-needed rest day before we would set out again towards the summit, which dominates the surroundings at 20,310 feet (6,190 meters). I gazed around at the snow-covered peaks all around us. They were magnificent, and I knew it was a sight very few people in the world have the chance to behold. It was hard to fully appreciate the beauty, however, because something was not right in my body. I was feeling dizzy and nauseated, and I had a headache that was getting progressively worse. I was experiencing the initial sensations and warning signs associated with the onset of Acute Mountain Sickness (AMS).

AMS is the mildest form of altitude sickness, a phenomenon that results from rapid exposure to low-pressure environments. The higher we climb, the thinner the air becomes, resulting in less oxygen available for our lungs in each breath. Blood vessels constrict and other physiological changes take place, triggering the production of red blood cells as our bodies adapt to the new environment. This process is usually accompanied by headaches, nausea, dizziness, loss of appetite, vomiting, and other unpleasant sensations.

The interesting thing about altitude sickness that continues to puzzle high-altitude researchers is that some people seem to acclimatize more slowly than others. For this reason, it is critical to be attuned to biological feedback in order to recognize when you are progressing into the altitude too quickly, so that you can make adjustments before it is too late. You need to stress your body in order to trigger the acclimatization process and red blood cell production, but too much stress can result in pulmonary edema, where fluid leaks into your lungs, or cerebral edema, where fluid leaks into your brain, both of which can eventually be fatal.

The howling wind at High Camp is intense and can escalate rapidly to the point where it blows tents off of the mountain or rips them to shreds, so we built snow walls around our tent to provide some shelter. I had also prepared some fortification against the storm within: I had researched AMS a fair bit and was monitoring my symptoms as well as consulting with my father. I was also drinking as much water as I could, a practice that helps speed up the acclimatization process, and eventually my headache and other altitude symptoms stabilized at a level that was still manageable.

The following morning my father and I both felt significantly better, so we departed on our push towards the summit. After scaling the harrowing Denali Pass and climbing for most of the day, we finally reached the summit. It was incredible to stand at the peak with my father and to have reached our end goal.

Knowing Yourself

When I speak at conferences and include parts of my family's expedition on Mount Everest in my message, one of the most common questions that I get when I open the floor up to questions afterwards is "Why?" As in, "Why on earth would anyone want to put themselves through such a climb?" Others in the audience usually chuckle or nod in agreement.

It is a valid question. George Mallory, to whom I am distantly related, was asked this same question by a reporter back in 1923 before his final, and ultimately fatal, attempt on Everest with his climbing partner, Sandy Irvine. He answered with what have become the most famous three words in mountaineering: "Because it's there."

I've also asked myself many times why I climbed Everest. I think ultimately my answer is "Because I'm here."

For me, climbing Mount Everest was a journey of self-discovery. There have been times in my life that I have put myself through other unique challenges for similar reasons of self-discovery. I suppose my own curiosity plays a major role in this. It is a curiosity to uncover personal truths and gain a better understanding of the limits of my own mental and physical abilities.

You could argue that there are safer and less arduous ways of self-discovery, and that's a valid point. But do we really know the depths of our strengths and weaknesses without putting them to the test? I wanted to know if I could actually push my mind and body to that limit and be successful in the end. And there's only one way to find out.

You may think you know yourself. After all, you *are* yourself. But you probably don't know nearly as much about yourself as you think. You know yourself like someone who lives on a mountain knows that mountain. They know where they live, but they probably don't know all of the mountain's ridges and valleys and trees and streams, and they've likely never seen it from a distance either.

This is your first summit: self-knowledge. You start by surveying and better understanding the mountain you're on.

Having a greater self-awareness allows us to act more consciously, rather than passively reacting to everything life throws at us. Self-awareness is becoming aware of our needs, skills, interests, values, hopes, dreams, beliefs, thoughts, actions, and other important characteristics that shape our existence. Without knowing where we are currently, what we have already tried, and what has shaped our reality, it's hard to know where to turn next. Since we mature and change throughout our lives, it's a continuous process, and we need to be forever updating and improving the knowledge and understanding we have about ourselves.

Just as I needed to know what was going on with my body as I sat at High Camp on Denali. I needed to recognize what I was feeling, and why.

What Are You Feeling?

You can't understand yourself unless you recognize and understand what you're feeling and what's causing it. I use the words *emotions* and *feelings* somewhat interchangeably throughout this book, but they're technically not the same thing. Feelings are sensations experienced consciously in terms of a subjective response, whereas emotions are much deeper; they can be conscious or unconscious, and they often affect our thinking and behavior—and cause many physiological responses—without us necessarily being able to consciously process or identify what is going on.

Emotions are part of a feedback loop with our thoughts and actions. We need to be able to accurately interpret our emotions to guide our decisions and actions. We are "experiencers" above all, and our emotions are the response to the experiences that we encounter throughout life. They guide our relationships and our decisions. And without our emotions, everything would be as dull as staring at a blank wall—perhaps even duller, since even emptiness often evokes emotion.

Philosophers used to view emotions as obstacles: disconnected, unexplainable emergences, interfering with and distracting from rational thought. The ancient Greeks thought that we needed to block out our emotions in order to be able to think clearly and make good judgments. So do many people in our own times.

There is a partial truth in this. Emotions can cloud or hijack our judgment—especially when we don't understand what we are feeling and why. It's tempting to try to suppress our emotions so that we can think and act with a calm, cool, and collected rationality. However, recent experiments in psychology, behavioral science, and neurobiology have shown that rational thought is impossible without our emotions.

Neuroscientist Antonio Damasio pioneered much of the research around understanding the role of emotions in decision-making. He developed the somatic marker hypothesis, which proposes that decisions are guided by assessing the feelings and physiological changes associated with each envisioned alternative. Damasio had a patient, who he refers to as Elliot, who had undergone surgery to remove a tumor from his prefrontal lobe, leaving him with frontal lobe tissue damage and the inability to feel emotion. Elliot had been a successful businessman, but after the surgery he was plagued with poor decisions that spiraled his life into ruin, resulting in unemployment, multiple divorces, and other problems. Damasio recalls that even simple decisions like deciding between multiple appointment times or choosing which color of pen to use became lengthy deliberation processes for Elliot. His lack of emotions paralyzed his decision-making abilities. Our rational minds can generate alternatives and arguments, but decision-making requires our emotions to evaluate the significance, based on feeling. In essence, emotions are what make things matter to us as humans.

This has turned out to be a real problem in the development of artificial intelligence. We have done a pretty good job in developing robots that can perceive and understand the objective reality around them, but how do you program a computer to make decisions based on the perceived value of the alternatives? Machines don't have the emotions, or an equivalent circuitry, that allow for this type of value differentiation.

Like a lot of the concepts we will be exploring in this book, there is a balance that needs to be reached between how much we rely on our emotions to influence our behavior and how much we override our emotional tendencies with rational logic. If we are headstrong enough, we can override emotional motivations, but we have to be careful, since the enjoyment we get out of life is tied to our emotional experiences. Suppressing them may be good if we want to be a cold, hard logic machine in making objective financial predictions, for example, but it is done at the expense of experiencing a meaningful life. And sometimes things can start to go very wrong, and you won't know how to deal with them. Pay close attention to your emotions: they tell you that something meaningful has happened or something has changed in your life. And they can guide your future directions by how you feel about different imagined scenarios.

Become Your Own Therapist

I am, in this book, in a way, asking you to become a therapist for yourself, even if you also work with a therapist. The first thing I mean by that is that you have to listen to yourself.

A good therapist spends as much time, sometimes even more time, listening to patients as they spend sharing ideas. In fact, some therapy sessions are almost entirely the client relaying their own story and challenges with the therapist simply lending an open and understanding ear. Surprisingly, there is tremendous benefit in this, even if this therapist doesn't say a word. This is what is often referred to as getting things off of one's chest. By talking, we are helping to discover more about ourselves and organize our thoughts and emotions. Verbalizing is an integral part of thinking, and by putting our thoughts into careful speech we are doing the required work to gain clarity.

When we are learning about ourselves on our own, we don't have a therapist listening to us, but if we're willing to listen to ourselves without judgment and without immediately reacting according to our programmed beliefs and preconceptions, we can learn a lot about ourselves. If we ask ourselves deep, meaningful questions, we often get deep, meaningful answers.

As we are exploring self-awareness, though, we need to know the difference between *internal* self-awareness and *external* self-awareness. In this book, I'm focusing primarily on internal self-awareness, which is improved through deep introspection and asking ourselves the right questions. Internal self-awareness is about clarity in knowing our own values, personality, passions, feelings, strengths, weaknesses, aspirations, and other important personal characteristics. In my view, internal self-awareness is the more critical component for personal growth. But we run the risk of developing distorted or unrealistic ways of viewing ourselves, especially if we have underlying mental health issues. This is where external self-awareness comes in, which allows us to calibrate our perspectives.

External self-awareness is about clarity in knowing how *other* people see us. We shouldn't define ourselves through the lenses of others, but we are social beings, and others can see things about us that we can't or won't. We need to be willing to ask for honest and constructive opinions from others and to be open to listening and learning in order for us to improve our external self-awareness.

And neither kind of self-awareness automatically leads to the other kind. Organizational psychologist Tasha Eurich has completed a lot of interesting research on self-awareness and has found that there doesn't seem to be much of a correlation between these two types of self-awareness. Since we want to bring our internal and external self-awareness into alignment, we need to work on both.

The Big Five Personality Traits

We can't know everything about mountains by measuring aspects of them, but we can know a lot. We know, for instance, that because the summit of Everest is 29,032 feet (8,849 meters) above sea level, there is only about a third as much available oxygen compared to sea level, since the lower pressure at altitude results in more dispersed oxygen molecules. We know that at High Camp on Denali, at 17,200 feet (5,242 meters), there is about half as much available oxygen as at sea level.

Likewise, we can know a lot about people's minds by measuring aspects of them. This is what *psychometrics* does; it's the theory and technique of psychological measurement. Psychometrics allows us to understand personality and other psychological traits numerically, which adds a degree of structure to what are otherwise extremely complex and nuanced concepts.

While there are various personality assessments available, almost all modern personality research is based on what are known as the Big Five personality traits, sometimes referred to as the Five Factor Model or OCEAN model. The Big Five model wasn't built from a particular psychologist's theory like most of the other personality assessments. It was developed from empirical data, which is one of the aspects that make it so credible.

Independent researchers discovered the same five broad personality dimensions through statistical analysis of personality questionnaires, using computers to factor analyze the data. What a factor analysis does is look at the similarities between questionnaire responses in order to determine how many factors are really being asked about. In a hundred-question questionnaire, there may be twenty questions that are worded differently but tend to get similar responses from any given respondent, which indicates they're really measuring the same aspect of personality. For example, question one may be something like "I enjoy spending time in large social groups" and question eighteen may be something like "I feel energized after attending a party." Although these are two different questions, they are really asking about the same personality trait, in this case extraversion. A respondent who ranked the first question as a 5 would also likely rank question eighteen as a 5. A factor analysis determines how many distinct factors there are, and it turns out in the case of personality that regardless of the questionnaire, there are five major traits: openness to experience, conscientiousness, extraversion, agreeableness, and neuroticism. Each trait is a continuum, and every one of us falls somewhere along each continuum. (Each trait also has subcategories, but I'll leave those aside for now.)

Studies have repeatedly correlated many life outcomes with these five traits—academic performance, marital stability, longevity, well-being, spirituality, health, psychological well-being, artistic preferences, income, relationships, happiness, and many more. These correlations are not only helpful as predictors, they also allow us to better understand and resolve interpersonal and personal challenges. What follows is a short summary of each of the traits, since I will be referring back to them. I've included a chart for you to refer back to as you progress through this book— and after.

THE BIG FIVE PERSONALITY TRAITS

LOW SCORE			HIGH SCORE
	• Cautious • Practical • Conventional	**OPENNESS** Creativity Intellect Ideas	• Curious • Inventive • Independent
−	• Disorganized • Impulsive • Careless	**CONSCIENTIOUSNESS** Diligence Self-discipline Responsibility	• Organized • Goal-oriented • Dependable **+**
	• Solitary • Reserved • Withdrawn	**EXTRAVERSION** Energy Talkativeness Assertiveness	• Outgoing • Energetic • Adventuresome
−	• Critical • Uncooperative • Detached	**AGREEABLENESS** Friendliness Cooperativeness Trust	• Helpful • Trusting • Compassionate **+**
	• Confident • Even-tempered • Resilient	**NEUROTICISMS** Negative emotion Emotional instability	• Nervous • Sensitive • Depressed

Adapted from J.M. Digman and L.R. Goldberg

OPENNESS TO EXPERIENCE is the trait associated with creativity, intellect, curiosity, and the flow of ideas. It describes the tendency to think in abstract, novel, and complex ways. Individuals low in openness are practical, conventional, cautious, and prefer routine; individuals high in openness are curious, have many interests, and are independent and open to change.

CONSCIENTIOUSNESS is the trait associated with self-discipline, responsibility, and dependability. Aside from IQ, conscientiousness is the strongest predictor of life success overall and has shown repeatedly in studies to also be a significant predictor of longevity. Individuals low in conscientiousness are impulsive, careless, and disorganized; individuals high in conscientiousness are goal-oriented, dependable, and organized. Conscientiousness can also be thought of as an individual's ability and inclination towards delaying gratification for future pay-offs at the expense of what feels good in the here and now.

EXTRAVERSION is the trait associated with how one's energy level is influenced by people and external stimuli. It describes the degree of assertiveness and enthusiasm that people exhibit, especially with respect to friendship, attention, and social status. Individuals who are low in extraversion are referred to as introverts. Introverts are quiet, solitary, reserved, and withdrawn; highly extraverted individuals are outgoing, warm, energetic, adventuresome, and get energized from spending time with others.

AGREEABLENESS is the personality trait associated with cooperation, trust, and compassion. It describes a person's propensity towards putting others' needs first and choosing cooperation over competition. Individuals low in agreeableness are critical, detached, uncooperative, and suspicious; individuals high in agreeableness are helpful, friendly, trusting, and easy to get along with.

NEUROTICISM is the trait associated with negative emotion and emotional instability. It describes how prone a person is to feeling sadness, fear, anger, guilt, frustration, loneliness, anxiety, and other negative emotions. Individuals low in neuroticism are calm, confident, even-tempered, and secure; individuals high in neuroticism are anxious, sensitive, negative, and unhappy.

There are stable aspects of our personality traits across our lifespans, but some traits do evolve as we mature, based on social factors and conscious efforts to make changes. These conscious efforts are particularly important. For example, I am naturally an introvert, but I found that this predisposition didn't align well with my broader goals in life and the person I wanted to become, so I have worked hard on becoming more extraverted through intentional changes to my thought patterns and behaviors. I now score relatively high in the trait of extraversion. But it is hard to say how deep this change goes: I seek out social interactions nowadays and genuinely enjoy such events, but there is still a part of me that also finds crowded social environments exhausting when I am in them for extended periods. I need to retreat in order to recharge, which suggests I'm still an introvert by nature.

It is also important to realize that there are both advantages and disadvantages associated with a high or low score for each of the traits. For example, I score relatively low in the trait of agreeableness. That may sound negative, but ends up being advantageous when it comes to business interactions and career advancement. Agreeable people on average get paid less than less agreeable people because agreeable people don't push and compete as much for wages and advancement. But it's a disadvantage in other situations, because I tend to be more argumentative and am prone to relationship friction, so I have more difficulty forming and maintaining friendships and relationships—although there are other personality factors that play a role in both of these areas that also need to be considered.

There doesn't appear to be an optimal personality distribution for all situations. But, depending on your chosen vocation and ambitions throughout life, some personality traits will be more advantageous than others for your specific purposes. This is where identifying and understanding your personality distribution is both informative and practical. Knowing what your strengths and weaknesses are allows you to capitalize on your strengths and, even more importantly, purposefully work on areas where you need to make improvements.

What You Know for Sure

"It's not what we don't know that gets us in trouble, it's what we know for sure but just ain't so." Everyone knows Mark Twain said this, except he probably didn't. But that's no trouble: there's a lot of truth in it, no matter who we're quoting.

Once we have made up our mind about something or held a belief for a period of time, we tend to rationalize and defend our thinking rather than consider alternatives. We interpret information through a preprogrammed lens, and we have perception biases that make us believe we are thinking and acting objectively when really we are not. This is why, as much as I can, I try to counter my perception bias and keep an open mind by asking myself, "If I had been raised in different circumstances, educated in different ways, and exposed to a completely different culture, would I think differently about this?"

Religion gives us a glimpse of just how important beliefs really are to us as humans. It should be self-evident that not all of the roughly 4,300 different religions around the world can be objectively true, since almost every one of them contradicts and even outright condemns the others. In spite of this, followers of each religion are certain that their beliefs are the absolute truth, so much so that many followers are willing to, and sometimes do, lay down their own lives or take others' lives in the name of their beliefs.

And yet those beliefs may not even really be theirs. The majority of our beliefs, especially religious ones, are almost completely instilled in us by others. It is possible for a person to carefully consider and choose their own religious beliefs, but 80 to 90 percent of people adopt the same religious beliefs as their parents. Yet, incredibly, we like to cling to the notion that our beliefs are our own, and it turns out that there are psychological reasons for this. Long-held beliefs become an integral part of us, and we protect them as fervently as we do the components of our physical body, sometimes even more so.

But this is not limited to religious beliefs. We have countless beliefs about all aspects of ourselves, the world, the universe, reality itself, and beyond, that we have developed and accepted based on many different factors. When my kids were very young, it intrigued and amused me to watch how they would carefully observe my facial expressions and reactions, and those of my wife, to determine the correct reaction to events, and even the acceptable reaction to their own actions. When something unexpected would happen, such as a dog barking or a plate breaking on the floor, our kids would immediately look up at us and try to determine the correct response. They would mimic our reactions, and eventually it became automatic. In our early years, this is how beliefs are formed: through observation of others.

Even in adulthood, everyone seems to have an opinion on how we should look, what we should wear, how we should feel, where we should work, how much we should make, where we should travel, what we should support, and so on. This is what socialization is all about, and it is difficult to determine to what degree this socialization influences our self-concept and our outward views. These are all things we need to understand on a deeper level when we're getting to know ourselves.

It's not that our beliefs are necessarily wrong. Even religious beliefs may be very well founded. But if we don't take a step back and better understand what is behind the many different aspects of our lives, we let ourselves become puppets of the social structures and world around us, and we're guilty of the same blind acceptance as the perpetrators of atrocities who are simply following the unquestionable teachings of their leaders. Don't be afraid to question everything—including what I say in this book.

Cognitive Defusion

How do we step back and observe our beliefs critically? One technique I have used many times is cognitive defusion, a concept originally developed by Steven Hayes. Cognitive defusion

is an excellent technique for discovering things about yourself, because the concentration is on observation rather than
judgment, analysis, or engagement. It is a little bit like active
listening, except you're practicing it with yourself and your own
thoughts. This technique ended up being one of the most significant and effectual tools that I employed in my recovery from
anxiety and depression. Once I got good at it, I was able to put it
into practice fairly quickly and in almost any situation.

The essence of cognitive defusion is allowing thoughts to
come and go, observing them but not judging, analyzing, or
reacting to them. In this way, you can emotionally disconnect
from your thoughts and not allow them to dominate or hijack
your mental energy and behavior. When I practice cognitive
defusion, I often add my own mental imagery as well, to guide
the technique. For example, I envision each thought floating into
my mind as a bubble or whisper through my right ear, notice
the thought while it is present inside my head, and then watch
it float out of my mind through my left ear. Once I have pic-
tured the thought floating away, I bring my attention back to my
open mind and await the next thought, which I picture floating
through my mind in the same way. This allows a degree of emotional detachment from my thoughts —especially those that I do
not want to be thinking about.

Sometimes I have taken the technique a step further: I will
sample my thoughts, as though I were a lawyer deciding on
whether or not to take on a new case. I take a few seconds to
superficially analyze whether or not each thought is one I want
to devote mental resources to or will be beneficial to me. If so, I
consciously choose to churn through the thinking for a certain
amount of time; if not, I let the thought float out of my head.

I have found this technique to be tremendously helpful, much
more so than trying to avoid or eliminate thoughts. When I
started on my mental health journey, I tried to practice clearing
my mind of all thoughts and images; I would envision my mind
as a movie screen, mentally wiping away anything that showed
up on it. But I just kept having to wipe away the same thoughts

and images over and over again, of whatever was bothering me at the time. Our thought patterns have become automatic from years of conditioning; turning them off isn't a viable option. You might as well try not to think about pink elephants—they'll be all you can think of.

Taking a step back from our thoughts and seeing them for what they are, as automatic thoughts that may or may not be true or helpful, is tremendously beneficial in decreasing rumination and anxiety. It takes practice, but the journey is worth it—especially if you find yourself frequently lost in your own rumination of negative thoughts.

Start Climbing

You can't get to the summit just by sitting and thinking about what route to take, however. You have to climb, and you can't always avoid the tough parts of the route. I have found that when I have the courage to ask myself deep, meaningful questions and really think about the answers without jumping to conclusions, I often discover or refine truths about myself. I have often had to ask myself tough questions in business negotiations about whether I'm being honest and whether decisions are in alignment with my moral compass. In deciding whether and how to write this book, I also had to ask myself some tough questions. What do I have of value that I can offer? How much of my life am I willing to share with the world? Am I being completely honest with myself? Why do I want to write this book to begin with?

I recommend you go through a similar process in your own life. Keep digging deeper to discover what endeavors and vocations are fulfilling and make you feel complete. Sometimes such realizations require simply trying out different paths and paying attention to how they make you feel, but you can often get answers to tough questions about yourself by letting your conscious and subconscious minds sift through your past experiences and how they made you feel. Ask yourself questions about your friendships and relationships as well. Do you feel a deep connection? Is there anything about the relationship that needs to change? Perhaps most importantly, ask yourself what you need to change or improve about yourself in order to become all you can be. Sometimes you will be surprised at the answers.

To climb towards the Summit of Self-Knowledge, you also need to be in good shape, and I mean that literally. This book focuses primarily on psychological well-being, but don't forget that there is a strong link between psychological and physical well-being. If you neglect your body, you drag your mind down as well.

When I don't get enough sleep for two or three nights in a row, for example, I can pretty much predict that I will get sick, as it seems to happen every time. When I've been on the road for a while and have been eating at fast-food restaurants or skipping meals altogether, I feel unwell physically and psychologically. When I haven't exercised for three or four days, I can get into a slump. I have been through periods of my life where I have surrendered to this state of lethargy. To regain my energy, I have often tried resting or taking naps, but the solution is counterintuitive: it is getting back into exercise that energizes me.

So if you are serious about making psychological improvements in your life, be wary of sabotaging your efforts by neglecting your body. Establish an exercise and nutrition routine that will keep you in good shape physically so that you can focus on your mind without adding additional stress and complications.

One more thing. Something Steve Jobs called "more powerful than intellect." Something even Albert Einstein called "the only real valuable thing." Intuition.

Intuition is a mysterious concept, difficult to identify and measure scientifically, although most of us seem to know it exists through personal experience. We have all experienced the soft inner voice or gut feeling that nudges us towards or away from a decision, without telling us why or how we will get there. Some people refer to this as their sixth sense, an inkling, a hunch, or their deeper instinct.

Intuition isn't really what we would refer to as insight, since the knowledge from insight is explainable, and with insight we gain clarity about an idea or solution. Rather, intuition is about sensing or feeling the direction we should take on a decision or problem. It's hard to pin down rationally, which is what makes it such a peculiar and perplexing phenomenon that has intrigued philosophers and psychologists for centuries. And yet we can't—or shouldn't—ignore it.

There have been times in my life when I have failed to follow my intuition, and I have generally regretted doing so. For example, the first home that Natalie and I owned was in Arizona, where we lived for almost two years. When we decided to move back to Canada, we put our house on the market. Within the first day, we received a number of offers above our asking price, and our realtor convinced us to take the highest offer right away, as it was an investor he knew and we wouldn't likely get an offer that high if we turned it down and waited. We signed the deal, even though it didn't feel right. We ended up receiving higher offers later on once it was too late. And the whole idea of selling the house never quite felt right in general. I allowed fear of the unknown and rationalization to override my intuition, and we have lamented our decision to sell ever since. Natalie and I have said to each other many times how much we would love to still have a place in Arizona to visit, and our house there has subsequently more than tripled in value.

Within our current understanding, it seems that intuition is a signal from our unconscious mind that does not require analytical reasoning or deliberation. Our unconscious mind rapidly analyzes our past experiences, outcomes, and aggregated knowledge, much of which is no longer consciously accessible through memory, to influence our decision-making. There is reasoning applied at the unconscious level in developing such intuition, but the reasoning is not conveyed to our conscious, only the intuition is.

In Western society, we're often inclined to suppress our intuition in favor of logic and reason, but we have to remember that intuition, too, plays an important role in the mind of the self-aware individual.

Intuition is separate from emotion, although it can be difficult to differentiate, especially without adequate practice and careful observation. As a general rule, intuition is more of a detached sensation that is less emotionally charged and feels like the right decision in our gut.

If you want to truly know yourself, listen to your intuition, learn from it, and respect it. Being in touch with your intuition is perhaps the cornerstone of self-knowledge.

Expedition Debrief

What are the key ideas from this chapter that you can extract and use in your own life? One of the early discoveries I made was that I didn't know myself nearly as well as I thought I did, and I think if you're honest with yourself you'll come to a similar conclusion.

Begin by taking an objective look at your belief systems. Try to deduce where they came from and the effect they have had on the trajectory of your life. You will find you have many long-held beliefs about yourself, your purpose in the world, your value, your abilities, the degree to which you control your own destiny, and more broadly about the universe and existence as we know it. Some of these beliefs may be serving you well but some may be incredibly self-limiting and troublesome. You may need to ask yourself tough questions along the way, but don't be afraid to challenge your beliefs in your quest to discover new truths.

How much have you learned about your own personality? I recommend taking a Big Five personality assessment to better understand the strengths and weaknesses associated with your trait distribution. There are many free online assessments that will give you good start. Knowing your strengths is an asset, but once you know what your potential shortcomings are, you also know where you can focus your development.

Do you find you are often ruminating on unwanted thoughts that seem foreign and automatic? Practice the cognitive defusion technique in order to learn to dissociate yourself from automatic thought patterns, many of which have been instilled in you throughout your upbringing. The space you create between yourself and these thoughts will allow you to be more observant and objective in making personal discoveries.

Are you sabotaging some of your best psychological efforts by neglecting your physical well-being or other areas of your life? Remember as you move through this book that all aspects of your being are closely connected. Although avalanches are generally triggered near the top of the mountain, their impact is felt all the way to the bottom.

THE SUMMIT OF SELF-MOTIVATION

Two Kinds of People

Years ago, I helped design a mechanical curling-stone launcher, worked on a backpack durability test machine, and upgraded a pool-playing robot known as Deep Green. It was all part of my undergraduate studies in mechanical engineering at Queen's University in Kingston, Ontario. The university had integrated theoretical knowledge with a lot of hands-on projects that were usually structured as real-world applications and challenges for students to solve. In most cases, my classmates and I were randomly assigned to work in small groups, so I had the opportunity to work with a wide range of other engineering students. And what became particularly apparent to me was the vast differences in my teammates' levels of motivation when it came to completing the work and compiling the reports and other deliverables we were required to submit.

At times, I was assigned to work with one or more individuals who were so full of energy and excitement in their pursuits that they seemed unstoppable. They would fly through the various tasks without complaint or hesitation, radiating positive energy in their wake. Their internal drive and momentum to achieve what they had set out to accomplish in university—and, it seemed, more broadly in life—was an unshakable force to be reckoned with.

But, perhaps more often, I was also grouped with students who seemed to lackadaisically float through each day, mindlessly waiting for things to happen to them and doing the bare minimum in order to avoid a failing grade. Their internal drive seemed to be completely and utterly lacking—the flame of their motivation had been mostly, if not entirely, snuffed out. Even a mechanical curling-stone launcher wouldn't have gotten them very far.

This dichotomy of motivation became even more apparent when I started working in industry as an engineer. Some of my coworkers were productivity powerhouses who eagerly took on new work without any external prompting, but there were quite a few that nearly had to have a fire lit under their chair to get them moving. Naturally, there were engineers closer to the midpoint between the two extremes as well, but I tend to remember the outliers most.

What constitutes the difference between these two kinds of people? That's the million-dollar question that managers, psychologists, sociologists, and many others have been grappling with for... well, millennia. And the mystery is far from solved. But we have learned some things about motivation—the summit we're going to plot a route to in this chapter.

If there's a Summit of Self that really brings to mind literal summits, self-motivation is it. Mountain climbing is so often used as a metaphor for motivation and achieving goals because it exemplifies the preparation, the challenge, the ambition, and the upward commitment required of us in many of the endeavors we find ourselves facing in life. And while this summit is important for achieving many other summits—we'll come back to it again and again later in the book—it's not a lesser peak. In fact, it's one of the most significant.

Why do we do the things we do? Not just because they're there. In the simplest sense, we do them because we want to. We want something, or we want to avoid something. But it is one thing to force yourself to begrudgingly and unhappily work through an activity and bring it to completion, and an entirely different, and certainly more desirable, thing if you can make experiential and psychological adjustments to the point where you are actually excited and content working through it. This is the real objective.

Extrinsic Motivation

I had a surprising learning experience about my own motivations a few years back. It had only been a couple of years since I started my own business, and I was quite focused on making ends meet, since I was now fully reliant on my own entrepreneurial ability in generating revenue. I had set a rather ambitious goal for myself that particular year, one that was at the limit of what I thought I could achieve. I made a plan, implemented it, and worked hard, pushing myself to persist and continually strive to do more in spite of many setbacks. And I surpassed my financial goal! But... so what?

I was bewildered. I thought that when I reached my goal I would feel a huge sense of pride and accomplishment, but to my surprise, that wasn't the case at all. Instead, I would describe what I felt as closer to "Meh."

It got me thinking long and hard about what motivates me. There must be something else in my work, something deeper, that excites and inspires me. Is it the challenge? Is it making a difference? Is it recognition? Perhaps it is the freedom and excitement of controlling my own direction?

This got me thinking as well more broadly about what I really want in life, and more generally about what most of us are striving for deep down. If we think more money or more power or more fame will make us happy and fulfilled, we're most likely chasing an illusion. We're following an *extrinsic motivation*: something outside ourselves.

And sometimes we're not moving *towards* anything. We're moving away from something, or being forced to move through *coercion*. Coercion persuades an individual or group by presenting a threat or other negative consequences for noncompliance. Nobody can actually *force* another person to do something, but if the consequences for not doing it are cruel enough, they can be motivated to comply. And this is the most obvious problem with coercion: many forms of coercion either directly violate human rights or run dangerously close to doing so. History is tainted with countless disturbing examples of how human beings have relied on threat and punishment to control other human beings, from slave drivers and gladiators to prisoner-of-war labor camps and sweatshops. But coercion is also used in more subtle ways everywhere around the world and all the time. If you have been threatened with having your pay cut, or losing time off, or being transferred to an undesirable job, or being fired, you have been coerced.

This doesn't mean coercion is always bad. An employer is well within their rights to threaten to fire someone if they refuse to comply with ethical standards of fairness and honesty, for example. But it can be tempting for people in positions of power to take coercion too far. Humans are not machines and shouldn't be treated as such.

When I was still working as an engineer, at one point I was involved in a research and development initiative relating to better methods of ore extraction. I was looking at a wide range of different concepts and assessing their viability through initial calculations and basic feasibility modeling. Early on in the project, one of my senior managers, who wasn't involved in the project but had been involved in my career development at times, came by my desk to check on what I was working on. I explained the project and what we were trying to accomplish as well as shared some of the initial concepts. He was intrigued and immediately offered his own solution to the challenge, so I wrote down his thoughts as one of the concepts to consider.

Over the next few weeks, I continued doing calculations and basic models, and, as it turned out, his concept, although good as an initial theory, did not have any viable application worth pursuing. Thus, I prioritized the concepts and shifted my efforts primarily to those that did look to be viable. A couple of weeks later, the same senior manager came by my desk again. He immediately asked about his design idea and how far I had gotten in developing it. I explained that I was focusing more on other designs that had more viability based on the initial calculations.

He started telling me a story about a young engineer who used to work near him years ago when the founder was still around and the company was in its infancy. The story seemed innocent at first, as he explained how the president of the company had come by one day smoking a cigar and casually shared with the young engineer an idea to develop. My senior manager continued, telling me that a few weeks later the president came back and found that the young engineer had not embraced the president's idea. He ended his story as he turned his back and began walking away by saying indignantly that he never saw that young engineer again.

That particular incident disturbed me, and I was admittedly angered for a period of time afterwards. On one hand, I was supposed to make decisions based on my knowledge and technical skills, yet on the other hand I was expected to blindly adhere to whatever ideas came down from above. This is the essence of coercion. I was being threatened in a pseudo-polite way to thoughtlessly implement my senior manager's idea or risk negative consequences. Was I intrinsically motivated and excited to work on the project after that incident? Was I excited and enjoying the initiative? Was I willing to put any more effort in than I was required to in order to retain my job? Of course not.

Herein lies the most fundamental problem with motivation through coercive force: there is generally zero *intrinsic* motivation present. In fact, people are often intrinsically moti-vated to rebel and do the exact opposite of what they are being coerced to do. They don't want to comply, they don't feel good about complying, and resentment takes the place of relationship building; furthermore, if the threat is ever reduced or removed, they will almost certainly stop complying entirely. External coer-cive force often makes the coercing individuals feel powerful, which is why it is so commonly used, but it is a fabricated power that primarily inflates one's ego and has very little depth in terms of true influence. Organizations and individuals that rely heavily on coercion to get things done are ultimately disadvantaged, and often doomed in the long run, because it is highly unlikely that any original ideas or improvements will come from this type of environment. It actively demotivates the people whose enthusi-asm and engagement are necessary for creativity and innovation.

Intrinsic Motivation

Later on in in my engineering career, I had the opportunity to work under our director of copper, who was a humble and empowering individual and a true pleasure to work with. No matter what level of the organization people came from, he treated everyone with respect and, in many ways, as equals.

Since we were working out of a satellite office, it was also possible for us to immerse ourselves in some really interesting projects with less risk of initiatives being snuffed out by hierar-chical layers of naysayers that were more concentrated in our head office. Thus, it presented a rare opportunity for me to get involved in some really innovative and challenging projects.

During that time, we learned of a challenge a smelter in Ari-zona was having with their emissions reduction efforts. Smelters are notoriously dirty in terms of off-gas emissions; this one was no exception, and I had been tasked with cleaning up the pro-cess. I was given the freedom to brainstorm solutions, so I came up with six rudimentary models, and before I knew it I was on a plane to Arizona to present the ideas. The client liked my initial solutions, and we ended up winning a contract to develop a working prototype that could be installed on one of their vessels.

When I worked on that project, I had *intrinsic* motivation. When I was engaged in my work, I often achieved what is referred to as a *flow state*, where I was so in the zone and engrossed in the details that it hardly felt like work at all. I would stay up half the night thinking about solutions and making sketches that I could model or implement the following day. Those aspects were primarily unpaid, since I completed the work at home as a result of the sheer interest and drive I had to find a successful outcome.

Interestingly enough, having seen the benefits of intrinsic motivation in myself, I've often tried to replicate this with the team members I've worked with since, but it's a difficult thing to achieve—it involves knowing another individual's deep-seated goals, ambitions, values, and what ultimately makes them tick. In my experience, the best a leader can do is to create a supportive and empowering environment that allows driven individuals to spread their wings and intertwine their own ambitions with the goals of the team or organization. This will not work for every team member, as some have very few ambitions to begin with or their ambitions are too removed from the work requested of them.

But when intrinsic motivation can be harnessed, genuine innovation and productivity are unleashed. When we look at almost all of the technological and humanitarian breakthroughs throughout history, they have arisen from intrinsically motivated individuals with a burning passion to succeed.

Carrots and Sticks

On a superficial level, your motivations may seem to come down to carrots and sticks: you have needs and wants that you hope to attain—carrots, aka *approach motivation*—and you try to avoid situations and actions that will put you in danger or cause you physical, psychological, or emotional harm—sticks, aka *avoidance motivation*.

In human terms, it turns out that we are really pursuing or avoiding the *feelings*, and there are relatively obscure ways that we derive these feelings. If you're like most of us, you are saying to yourself, "I do all kinds of things that don't make me feel good, but I do them because they need to be done!" It is true that we do pursue and complete things all the time that we don't particularly like to do: washing dishes, changing diapers, cleaning up after others... In these instances, it is important to realize that it is the anticipation of perceived feelings in *relative* terms, not absolute terms, that matters. In other words, we do these things because we believe that the feelings we will get by *not* doing these things will be worse than the feelings we will get by doing them. Diaper changing may not be enjoyable, but deep down we know that the screaming, bum rash, unpleasant smell, infection, anger from spouse, social judgments, eventual doctor visit, and other negative consequences that will come to pass by not doing the chore will be worse than just doing it.

In other words, we are motivated to act when the pain associated with inaction becomes greater than the pain associated with the action.

Advertisers understand very well just how motivated humans are by feelings, and they are cunningly effective in taking advantage of this fact. If advertisers can change the way we feel towards a product or service, it drastically changes our buying decisions, which is why the advertising industry's worth is now estimated at more than $1.2 trillion dollars.

Some desires are very basic and primal. And when basic survival needs are in jeopardy, humans and animals will do almost anything to try to survive.

On our ascent up Everest, my family and I left a partially filled oxygen cylinder at a section known as the Balcony—a small plateau at 27,500 feet (8,382 meters) in elevation. We were planning on making use of the oxygen on the way back down. But when we returned to it, there was a climber leaning up against a rock who had our cylinder in a death grip. He insisted that it was his, and he was not willing to relinquish it.

Basic needs trump everything. We are motivated to pursue basic needs in our lives mostly for survival and propagation: food, water, shelter, sleep, air, security, health, intimacy, and family. The psychologist Abraham Maslow put these types of needs at the base of his hierarchy of needs. Maslow suggested that human needs can be represented in a hierarchical order, often depicted as a pyramid, with our most basic physiological needs at the bottom. Above them are safety needs, then belongingness and love needs, then esteem needs, and, lastly, self-actualization needs at the top of the pyramid. We work to satisfy lower needs first before moving upwards.

MASLOW'S HIERARCHY OF NEEDS

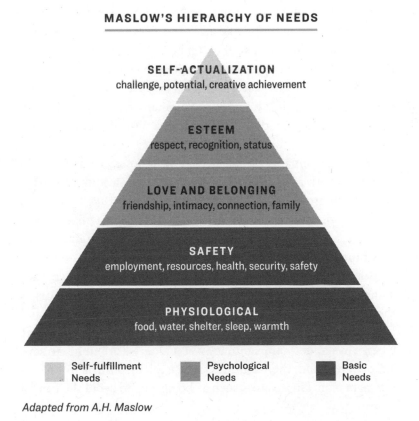

SELF-ACTUALIZATION
challenge, potential, creative achievement

ESTEEM
respect, recognition, status

LOVE AND BELONGING
friendship, intimacy, connection, family

SAFETY
employment, resources, health, security, safety

PHYSIOLOGICAL
food, water, shelter, sleep, warmth

Self-fulfillment Needs

Psychological Needs

Basic Needs

Adapted from A.H. Maslow

I don't need to dwell on the basic survival motivators. This book is focused on moving towards self-actualization, which is the top of the pyramid. But every mountain climber knows how much harder it is to climb without adequate nutrition, sleep, or, especially, oxygen. When you haven't been able to satiate, or at least partially satisfy, your basic needs, you aren't in a position to be motivated very much, if at all, by higher-order concerns. Which means, as I said in the Summit of Self-Knowledge chapter, you need to prioritize taking care of yourself before you are in a position to pursue other goals—including taking care of others.

Altruism

But what about altruism—the moral practice of selfless concern for the welfare of other people, even at the expense of one's own desires? For altruistic acts, there is believed to be no benefit to the individual. When parents give their lives for their children, when someone runs in front of a car to save a stranger, when people donate their life savings to humanitarian causes, when a person donates a kidney or even just a pint of blood, why do they do it?

From a personality perspective, a willingness to help others correlates with a high level of agreeableness, although extraversion and neuroticism also are factors. It seems that some of us are more wired for social concern, and it isn't immediately clear how much of this is rooted in our biology and upbringing versus how much is related to personal choice.

But in any event, if we do it, we *want* to do it, so we have some personal internal reward from doing it, right? This is the *psychological egoism* argument, and it is very difficult, if not impossible, to refute. From a psychological egoism standpoint, when a bystander jumps into icy water and risks their life to save a drowning child, their actions can be explained through subconscious personal motivators such as being able to avoid the pain of watching the child drown, dodging the personal guilt they would feel if they chose to do nothing, avoiding the public shame that could be directed towards them, receiving the potential recognition or thanks they may receive, and feeling the deep personal satisfaction of their own good deeds.

Cognitive research seems to support this: functional magnetic resonance imaging (fMRI) has been used to observe brain function during altruistic decision-making, and it turns out that some of the core processing regions of the brain that light up in terms of blood activation are the reward regions associated with pleasure. We could try to propose that the intentions are not based on the expectancy of a pleasure response, that the pleasure feelings are just a bonus, but this would be like claiming that the feeling of satiation we get after eating dinner does not influence our motivation to eat dinner in the first place.

Still, while it may be impossible to refute the psychological egoism argument empirically, it loses some credibility because it relies on circular reasoning. The argument that "All altruistic acts are inherently selfish because they satisfy the subject's inherent desire to act selflessly" is a chicken-and-egg problem, a causality dilemma: we are inherently selfish because alleviating our internal distress is what causes our desire to help others, but we are inherently selfless because our desire to help others causes the internal distress. The psychological egoism argument assumes that the reward is the motivation, not just the result— a logical fallacy: it relies on the very point it's trying to prove in order to prove the point.

The fact that we are motivated at least partially by the desire to alleviate our own negative emotions is probably disturbing for some, as it was for me, but where I still think altruism exists is in the desires themselves. If altruism is an illusion, why do some people have more of a desire to help other people in the first place? The desire is real and, in the end, the positive effect is still produced.

Compassion

A few years ago, there was a young child in a condominium not far from where we were living who had wandered outside alone one night wearing little more than a diaper. He was staying with his grandparents and had woken in the middle of the night, put on his boots, and left the condo, presumably to try to find his parents. It was the middle of winter and one of the coldest nights of the year. The building had an automatic front door that was motion-activated from the inside but locked from the outside. When he was discovered missing in the morning, the whole community started searching for him, and eventually his body was discovered, curled up lifeless under a nearby porch.

I felt sick to my stomach and teared up hearing the news, and it still bothers me even as I'm writing about it many years later. I desperately wanted to be able to do something to help, and yet there was nothing I could do.

From a motivation perspective, though, whose suffering did I want to alleviate in the end? Was it my own suffering? Was it the little boy's suffering? Was it the family's suffering? Was it the community's suffering? Perhaps it was all of these simultaneously. The "selfish" internal motivators and the "selfless" external motivators are fully integrated in a case like this. The motivation is truly both, and we cannot have one without the other.

Compassion and the actions resulting from compassion are probably as close as we can get to true altruism. The word *compassion* comes from Latin meaning "suffering together": the emotions that well up inside us when we are confronted with the thought, image, or real-life reality of the suffering of another being and are motivated to relieve the suffering. This last point is also what technically differentiates compassion from empathy. Empathy is when we are able to put ourselves in another person's shoes, so to speak, and feel their emotions. Compassion also includes the desire to do something about it.

Does the motivation come from genuine concern for the sufferer, which is what we like to believe, or a motivation to rid ourselves of the negative emotions associated with compassion by solving or improving the problem causing the suffering to begin with? We know that in the absence of our own emotions we feel indifferent about seeing suffering—or seeing anything else, for that matter. This has been demonstrated through patients with amygdala connection damage and other brain injuries, as we touched on in the Summit of Self-Knowledge. Without our emotions, the sight of a suffering child would motivate us no more than the sight of a rock. So, in the end, altruistic decisions and compassionate actions seem to be an integration of self-gratifying and selfless factors. And this seems to be the most realistic way of seeing them from a motivation perspective as well.

There are two reasons why this all matters here. The first is that it is relevant to the practical application of motivating principles, as we shall see throughout the remainder of this chapter. The primary reason, however, is to constrain any predisposition we may have towards self-righteousness and inflated moral virtue. We may be tempted to think of ourselves as better than those who are less altruistic, but before we give ourselves too much of a pat on the back, we have to realize that it isn't clear how much of our disposition to giving, in terms of both desire and derived pleasure, is actually a result of our own free choices and how much is a result of our genetically and nurture-derived personality distribution.

What is clear is that each of us has an internal motivation to act consistently within the bounds our own personal values. It causes us personal distress when we don't. And while some values may not be intrinsically better than others, some clearly are. There are actions that are morally wrong no matter what our upbringings have been. I think we all know and feel this deep down, and our parents and influencers, especially in early childhood, can do us a great moral disservice if they neglect to teach us right from wrong, not just through words but through discipline and role modeling. Our personal values—the ones that reward us when we do what we believe is right—need to orient us to what is actually right.

From a personality perspective, it should be no surprise that individuals who are higher in conscientiousness, particularly the sub-facet of orderliness, tend to be more motivated by personal value conformance. Personal value conformance has significant influence on many acts that we consider altruistic: Many people who have taken great risks to save others have said things like "I couldn't live with myself if that child had died." People throughout history have often gone through extreme personal turmoil or even taken their own lives after they have failed to do what they feel they should have done in moral instances. Some people would sooner literally die than fail to conform to their personal values.

A variant of personal value conformance is social value conformance, which is more of a hybrid since there is overlap with some of the other internal motivators. We often refer to this as *honor*, and it has both a personal and social aspect in terms of motivation. We are motivated to maintain our honor by being faithful to customary values: family values, societal values, nation values, club values, religious values, and the many other types of social values that we blur with our own values.

Where things really get messy is when our personal values and social values are in conflict, which results in a psychological state referred to originally by psychologist Leon Festinger as *cognitive dissonance*. Cognitive dissonance also occurs when we take part in actions that violate our personal or social values, or even when our ideas and beliefs are contradictory. In these cases, we are highly motivated to make changes that bring consistency back in order to reduce the discomfort associated with cognitive dissonance.

I experienced cognitive dissonance while climbing on the Lhotse Face, for example, to Everest Camp 3.

During my ascent, I was approached by a climber who had gotten cerebral edema and was being quickly escorted to a lower altitude to try to avoid the imminent death that would otherwise ensue. The climber staggered up to me and deliriously mumbled, "Water... need water."

I was faced with a moral dilemma at that point: I knew I needed to retain the little water I had left in order to avoid ending up in a similar state, but I also knew I had the ability and resources to provide aid. The prospect of ignoring his plea to maximize my own chances of survival caused me psychological discomfort, since it was inconsistent with my moral compass, so I ended up giving him the last of my water. I rationalized my decision through the assumption that I would be able to melt additional ice and snow once I arrived at Camp 3, although that was really a downplaying of actuality in order to relieve my mental discomfort, as I did not know how far ahead of me the camp actually was.

Social Life

How people respond to us socially—and how we perceive them to have responded to us—matters. I say *perceive* because we frequently misinterpret social responses—and inaccurately anticipate them as well—because we're filtering them through our own preconceptions.

We like to tell ourselves that social recognition doesn't affect our decisions, such as when we give time or money to a charity, but numerous studies have shown otherwise. When charities increase public recognition, people give more money and hands-on support. To get quite a lot of money from someone, offer to name a building or other permanent structure or institution after them. Deep down most of us—and the rich no less than the poor—long to be looked on favorably from within our peer groups and by society in general. But we don't want others to think that social recognition is why we do things; we want to seem altruistic, and not needy. So we come up with all kinds of creative ways of obscuring the connection.

And as powerful as the need for social recognition and appreciation is, the need to avoid negative social judgment is even more powerful. In particular, people are most influenced by negative judgment avoidance when they are high in neuroticism and low in extraversion. I understand this fear well from the onset of my own mental health challenges. But this fear isn't a rarity: survey respondents consistently rank their fear of public speaking even higher than their fear of death.

Such is the strength of the dread of public shaming. Political events, professional associations, churches, and other social groups also take advantage of this to some degree when they have a collection of money during the meeting or service. There is an awkwardness and guilt felt by people if they pass the collection basket without throwing in a donation, and the public scrutiny, whether real or perceived, makes these feelings even more pertinent. You don't want to be seen as a taker; it is important to maintain social reciprocity.

Reciprocity is the social balance sheet. We expect an even give-and-take. This has been deeply ingrained in humans from the beginning, since even before we invented currency, and not just between individuals but between groups: tribes would exchange gifts of food, clothing, or other goods with neighboring tribes. There is a practical aspect to this, since giving as you can when the occasion calls for it helps ensure you are more likely to receive when you have the need. But there is also a goodwill aspect in terms of showing appreciation and establishing reciprocity conformance with another tribe or individual.

Not everyone upholds the unwritten rules of reciprocity to the same degree, of course. Some people allow other motivators, such as amassing of wealth, to override it. People who habitually break the unwritten rules of reciprocity and take without giving back are often referred to as leeches. Leeches especially take advantage of individuals who are high in agreeableness, particularly the politeness and compliance aspects. If that describes you, a life lesson will be learning to say no, to voice your frustration with the lack of reciprocal action, and to move on before the leeches suck the life and generosity out of you.

The reciprocity principle can also be invoked proactively, and very frequently is: "I scratch your back, you scratch mine." This is obviously not altruistic, since there is a clear hope of a return on investment, but we often do favors with the hope of return and yet try to convince ourselves and others that our motivations are purely altruistic.

Businesses know that social reciprocity can be worth money to them. Grocery stores provide tasting stations, department stores give out free samples of perfume, contractors take prospective clients golfing, vendors give Christmas baskets, charities include free packages of seeds when asking for mail-in donations, and free e-books or online courses come with a sales pitch at the end. And then there are timeshares.

Timeshare sales presentations are a paramount example of taking advantage of social reciprocity. Representatives from the company trying to sell timeshare vacation ownership will set up a stand, usually by the beach where the tourists are, and offer something "free." It has to be enough to attract attention—a couple of nights' stay, a show, an excursion, a meal, or some combination of these. The only catch is that the individual or couple accepting the gift on offer agrees to attend a presentation highlighting the company's newest properties. Natalie and I have attended a few of these, since I was curious about their tactics, and we enjoyed the freebies that went with our participation.

Once at the sales presentation, the salesperson applies many different persuasive strategies all at once, but one of the major ones is reciprocity. Not only have they given a significant gift up front, but at the presentation there is free food, free drinks, and other gifts. The salesperson then gives each prospective buyer a tour and sits down with them to go over the advantages. It is important that the whole process takes a good amount of time as well, since reciprocity motivation is also invoked when others have given us their time. And, lastly, the salesperson, or sometimes their sales manager, shows the prospective buyer the "regular price," and then explains they will lower the price significantly to a new value. Nothing physical has been given, but the perception is that the salesperson has made a concession, so the prospective buyer feels motivated to reciprocate by making the purchase. I've never bought a timeshare, since I've run the math and it has never made financial sense to me, but a good sales presentation sells a timeshare to one in four attendees, and almost nobody is planning to buy when they first agree to accept a free meal or night's stay.

The power of the reciprocity principle is why politicians and others in influential positions need to be very careful about accepting gifts. Even if they believe they will still act objectively in their decision-making, it is impossible not to be influenced by a motivation to reciprocate.

There are positive and negative manifestations of the reciprocity principle. On the positive side, reciprocity is correlated with our levels of agreeableness and conscientiousness. As you would expect, agreeable and conscientious people are more likely to be motivated to return favors and uphold moral agreements. The negative manifestation of the reciprocity principle is what we call vengeance, payback, or getting even: "an eye for an eye, and a tooth for a tooth." There is a feeling of satisfaction when justice has been dealt. Many judicial fines and punishments are essentially based on principles of reciprocity. And for a lot of people, especially those high in neuroticism, vengeance motivations can become horrible, almost-unstoppable internal drivers. Some people devote nearly their entire lives to acts of vengeance. Succumbing to negative reciprocity can consume you.

Gaining, Keeping, and Not Losing

When I was young, my grandfather used to tell me about the importance of a dollar. He had lived through the Great Depression and, like many in his generation who were called "penny pinchers" or "cheapskates," he was often focused on saving money everywhere he could. And he was relatively wealthy. But I knew him well, and I came to see that his financial motivator was not so much wealth generation as it was the fear of scarcity. His thriftiness was a defense mechanism for preparing for hard times, like a squirrel storing up nuts for winter; he spent very little on himself—he shopped at second-hand stores and looked for coupons and grocery sales to minimize expenditures.

The human motivation to amass wealth is probably the least altruistic motivator we'll be looking at. We look down on "greed" and "miserliness," and yet we value thrift, saving, and striving for financial success.

There are indeed several aspects to striving for, accumulating, and retaining wealth. First and foremost, before we even look at personal gain or satiation of desires, we are loss-averse creatures. Many psychological studies have shown that humans are much more motivated to avoid a loss of a certain magnitude than they are to pursue a gain of the same magnitude. This phenomenon was first identified by Daniel Kahneman and Amos Tversky in 1979 and eventually earned Kahneman the Nobel Prize in Economics in 2002. They called this model prospect theory.

Being able to save for the future is also a type of delayed gratification. It is healthy to develop this discipline, and we value self-control and the ability to forgo small gains in the present for larger gains in the future—even if we're not all always very good at it.

And there is the desire for reward, which is not always seen positively, especially when we see it as greed. But Victor Vroom's expectancy theory of motivation sheds some light on its value for motivation. Vroom postulates that humans will be motivated if they believe their efforts will lead to successful results and they will be rewarded for their success. Both these conditions need to be in place and, for exemplary motivation, people need to be able to clearly see the connection between effort, achievement, and reward. I particularly like Vroom's model, as it recognizes the need for any rewards given to be based on merit rather than on simply showing up, an important distinction we will cover more in later chapters.

Opportunity, reward, and the freedom to pursue them are deeply related to the meaning and positive emotion we get out of life. We feel confined, like caged animals, when we have these taken away from us. The pursuit of goals and the small successes along the way is one of the ways that we find fulfillment in life.

Competition

Competition can bring us the rewards of small successes, as my father once demonstrated in an entertaining way.

When my brother Adam and I were in high school, we constructed a large wooden jump that we used for knee-boarding behind our motorboat. It was about five feet wide and five feet tall, with three barrels underneath for flotation, and a carpet-covered ramp extending down underneath the water. The driver of the motorboat would zip by beside the jump, allowing the knee-boarder behind to cut the wake and fly off of the jump. It was incredibly fun.

After a few days of knee-boarding adventures, we moved the jump to the edge of the water at the base of a fairly steep hill. We had a rusty old BMX bike and had gotten into our heads the idea of riding it down the hill and off the jump. There were no seat or brakes on the bike, so it was a matter of standing on the pedals and holding on for dear life until you were airborne. If we did it right, we would propel ourselves fifteen or twenty feet out into the lake and throw the bike away in midair so as not to bump and bruise ourselves with it as we hit the water. We then had to dive down and retrieve the bike before swimming it back to shore. This, too, was great fun.

After Adam and I had ironed out most of the kinks in the process, we started egging our father on to see how far he could fly off of the jump. He was not crazy on the idea, but none of us liked to be outdone by the others, so before long he was hiking up the hill with the rusty BMX bike in hand.

The first time he started down the hill, his nerves got the better of him: he decided to abort the mission just before getting to the jump. He leaped off the bike and injured his ankle as he hit the ground, putting him out of commission for a week.

But the following weekend, up the hill he went again, bike in hand.

He didn't have the balance quite right, though, as he careened down the hill. We have a great photo of him flying through the air, fully upside down and partway through a backflip, with the BMX bike jettisoned above him.

Needless to say, that was the last time he volunteered to try the bike jump. He had risen to the challenge, and that was enough for him.

Competition can be a very powerful internal motivator, but not everyone is equally motivated to win. Some individuals even prefer to avoid competition completely and hold up the white flag of truce as soon as they are challenged. From the various psychological studies that have been carried out, it appears that individuals high in extraversion and conscientiousness are most likely to be motivated by competition. There is also a negative correlation between competition and agreeableness, which makes sense since those high in agreeableness are more prone to seeking cooperation.

Competition can be an extrinsic motivator, an intrinsic motivator, or a combination of both. Extrinsically, competition is about things like social recognition, winning a prize, monetary rewards, and gaining respect. Intrinsically, competition is about things like personal satisfaction, gaining strength or skills, and building confidence and enjoyment. When we win competitions, we get a rush of dopamine, which is the hormone that makes us feel good. Thus, we are more motivated to continue winning and to seek out further competition.

The thing with competition, though, is that only a few individuals win and almost everyone else loses. And if you're not good at something and can't seem to get better at it, perpetually losing can be very demotivating. But most competitive individuals are inspired by high achievers and are motivated to try to surpass them, which—when done through honest effort—is the positive manifestation of competition.

Personal Fulfillment

If, on the other hand, you compete with yourself—set yourself a challenge to overcome—and win, no one loses.

After I finished university, I got the notion in my head that I wanted to learn to ride a unicycle. It was a skillset that not many people had, and I thought it would be an interesting challenge. I borrowed a unicycle from a friend who had given up on it, and, in the evenings after work, I started my attempts at riding it. I soon found out, however, that it didn't go as I had envisioned.

I was renting a room from a guy who owned an apartment in a large condominium complex. At first, I just tried to sit on the silly thing in the hallway, holding the walls and rocking the pedals back and forth. Then I moved to the main hall of the building, where I could attempt a few pedal strokes before crashing into one of the walls or falling flat on my back. But I was damaging the walls every time I crashed into them. Eventually, I graduated to the underground parking garage. My continuous falls down there got quite painful since they were onto pavement instead of carpet, but I kept at it night after night. After what seemed like an eternity, I began to slowly get the hang of it; after many months, I was finally able to ride a unicycle.

The question is, though: Why would I want to learn to ride a unicycle in the first place? I asked myself this many times. There was obviously no economic benefit, since I wasn't interested in joining the circus. There wasn't any social recognition benefit, since most people I mentioned it to just rolled their eyes or laughed at the notion. It was useless from a transportation perspective—way too slow. It's not even seen as a prestigious sport or skill; it is primarily seen as a trivial prop for acrobats and clowns. I can't think of any motivation that drove me to learn to ride the unicycle other than to prove to myself that I could.

This seems to be what personal fulfillment is: a deep motivation to pursue something for the simple purpose of mastering it... because it's there, you could say, and because *you're* there. Like climbing mountains. It is hard to do a cost benefit analysis on a mountaineering expedition: the cost is significant, but the benefit—the personal satisfaction of reaching the peak—can't really be quantified.

From a personality perspective, fulfillment, and self-improvement in general, is most highly correlated with the trait of openness to experience. Open individuals are curious and are motivated to learn and to continue learning throughout life. This is my highest-scoring trait, so it makes sense that this is one of my most dominant motivators. I think fulfillment has played a major role in many of the pursuits and accomplishments that I have had in life.

Douglas McGregor's theory on motivation adds an interesting perspective on this internal motivator, and it seems we aren't all influenced to the same degree. McGregor determined that some workers have their nature defined by what he calls Theory X: they are inherently lazy, selfish, adverse to responsibility, and lacking ambition. Others, however, are defined by Theory Y: they are internally motivated, responsible, and enjoy bettering themselves though their work. His view is that managers need to take a top-down controlling, supervising, and intimidating approach to motivating Theory X workers, but focus on positive work environments, rewards, and encouragement for Theory Y workers.

I am less inclined to take such a binary approach to individuals. I opened this chapter talking about working with people who would fit into McGregor's X and Y types, but I don't think we can overlook some of the deeper factors that may be blocking or distracting Theory X workers from transitioning their behaviors to be more like Theory Y workers. Some people seem like Xs, but then something changes and it is like a light bulb is switched on. I have seen this with delinquent youth who are finally taken under the wing of a caring and empowering mentor. Their lives are often completely changed for the better and they exhibit new energy and passion that didn't seem to exist inside of them before their transformation.

Power and Control

"Power tends to corrupt; absolute power corrupts absolutely." Lord Acton said it, and history attests to it. It takes a very strong-willed person to resist the temptation of abusing power. Everyone thinks that if only they were in charge, they would be fair and benevolent in distributing the common good, but corruption inevitably takes hold.

From a personality perspective, studies have found that people who are high in the trait of extraversion are more likely to have corruption tendencies, particularly those that are also low in conscientiousness. It happens that extraversion is also a valued trait in politicians and other leaders, however, and conscientiousness can be an obstacle to advancement since conscientious individuals tend to follow the norm.

But this doesn't mean that all forms of power are bad. Power refers to one's ability to control or direct others and, although this can be gained through forceful means and corruption, it can also be gained through displays of legitimate competence and enhancing the lives of others. Consider Martin Luther King Jr., who had significant power to influence and direct his followers but used this power productively for achieving greater good.

And there are plenty of positive character traits that help people gain power, such as charisma, empathy, open-mindedness, and generosity. I don't see anything wrong with gaining this type of power—as long as there are internal and external forces to keep corruption at bay.

There is one more form of power and control, one that is more personally directed. This is what the self-determination theory of motivation refers to as autonomy. Autonomy is our motivation to control the course of our lives. This type of internal power and control is important to develop, and it is a positive characteristic, unless of course it is applied to the detriment of those around us. It is an important factor in self-actualization— which will be our seventh summit.

Affiliation and Cause

Psychologist David McClelland's Three Needs Theory identifies three primary needs, three motivating drivers, we have in life: achievement, power, and affiliation. Our achievement motivator is the need to demonstrate our own competence. Our power motivator is our need for prestige and impacting others. We've already looked at both of those. The third one is our affiliation motivator: our need for acceptance, love, and belonging. We tend to feel lost or disoriented if we do not have a sense of belonging in our lives.

One way we achieve this sense of belonging is by affiliating ourselves with larger social organizations. And while we can join just for the sake of being part of a group, our motivation is much greater if we are supporting a common cause. There is a deep human desire to be part of something that is larger than us. We can compound our impact and we can bolster our resolve by aligning ourselves with similar-minded individuals.

Effective organizations understand the importance that affiliation and uniting behind a common cause plays in people's lives. They strive to create atmospheres and opportunities for this to take place. Otherwise, people are often motivated to leave and find an organization where they feel like they do belong.

Affiliation also seems to be related to our wanting to be useful or, more accurately, to *feel* useful. It gives us purpose in life and cuts through some of the chaos. Individuals who are highly extraverted and high in agreeableness are most likely to be motivated by affiliation.

Supernatural Beliefs

The final internal motivator I want to touch on is the motivation associated with supernatural beliefs—religions, of course, but also psychic beliefs, superstitions, demons, ghosts, angels, witchcraft, other dimensions, or any number of supernatural phenomena. These beliefs don't rely on scientific proof, so the magnitudes of the associated motivations are based on the strength of individual convictions. As we've seen in the Summit of Self-Knowledge, motivations associated with supernatural beliefs are as strong as our basic survival motivations, and they can be both approach and avoidance motivators—religions give the promise of a reward for compliance and a punishment for deviation, and usually both of these are at the extremes.

Supernatural beliefs are reliable. We don't like chaos and uncertainty in our lives, and supernatural beliefs give us something solid and unshakable. Worldly possessions can be taken away, relationships can be shattered, ideas can be disproven, and loved ones can die, but supernatural beliefs provide a calm, consistent bedrock that quells all the storms that we encounter throughout life.

There is nothing inherently wrong with believing in the supernatural, and there are psychological benefits when such beliefs give people stability. The danger comes when the desires and agendas of the humans involved—especially the leaders— motivate followers to do things that harm themselves or others. The important thing is to be aware of our own motivations so that we can try to guard ourselves against these all-too-human interferences.

Motivating Yourself

When you know what moves you, you know how to move yourself. There is tremendous benefit in understanding motivations if you are going to be involved in endeavors like coaching competitive teams, managing projects, establishing healthy relationships, and leading service groups. But this book is about the summits of self—*your* self. Our focus is on the practical aspects of personal motivation.

The base of this mountain is your motivation to satisfy your basic needs. Your other motivations are tempered or obscured significantly when basic survival needs have not been met. When you're standing at 27,000 feet (8,230 meters) on a mountain, clinging to an oxygen canister, you won't be talking about timeshares.

We need to be careful about getting ourselves into situations where our basic needs are in jeopardy. For our ancestors, this would include failing to store away enough food for the year or not preparing shelters in the summer months to withstand the harshness of winter. Nowadays, it is more often finance or security related, and we don't always remember the difference between basic needs and basic wants. When we encumber ourselves with gigantic mortgages, car payments, lines of credit, unpaid credit card bills, and other liabilities, we end up being so overextended that we have very little room to focus on higher-order motivations.

When I was working as an engineer, there was a period when our primary business sector, mining and metal, was going through a significant slowdown, and a lot of layoffs were happening at a rapid pace. I can remember the morale around the office at that time, the tension hanging in the air like a thick fog. People were nervously looking around for who would be next to get a tap on the shoulder and dreading that they themselves would be the ones packing their boxes. There was one gentleman in our group who was particularly uneasy. He had just made a big house purchase and had borrowed money for numerous luxuries he was slowly starting to pay off. He was living paycheck to paycheck, and he knew he would lose it all if he was let go, so his anxiety level was through the roof. The ironic thing was that because he was so high-strung, his productivity declined to basically zero, which only served to accelerate his eventual termination.

I remember during that time being a little perplexed at how nonchalant I felt about the whole situation, especially compared to the tension built up all around me. I still had my own mental health challenges, so I had plenty of ups and downs from that, but I was surprisingly indifferent to the prospect of being laid off. I didn't have a huge amount of savings, but I had minimized loans and liabilities to almost zero, and I was confident in my ability to find another job if needed. It wasn't a survival-level matter of basic needs for me—nor even of basic wants.

And so it is. The individuals that I know who are happily focused on manifesting their aspirations in life and making a difference in the world around them have made sure that their foundational needs are taken care of before moving on to higher ambitions. Remember this if you are frustrated by your own lack of motivation in pursuing your dreams: You may need to start with fundamental problems to solve and work your way up to more monumental challenges. And if you are frustrated at other people not being motivated by things you believe to be important, look and see where they are with their more immediate basic needs.

It is also, as we have seen, not always a matter of cool, rational calculation. We are emotional and rational beings. We can force ourselves to do something through rational thinking, but that isn't the same as really wanting to do it. And when our rational thoughts and our emotions are opposed, unless we are particularly headstrong about an issue, our emotions usually win— and our rational mind might serve mainly to justify what we already want.

Personal Rewards and Penalties

We know that motivation is about what we want to have and to avoid—carrots and sticks. The most basic, physical level of this is rewarding and penalizing yourself.

In essence, you are establishing an agreement with yourself where, if you do complete the terms, you will reward yourself, or if you don't complete the terms (or succumb to negative terms), you will face penalties. But you have to know yourself well enough to know how and even whether this technique will work. It works best if you are high in conscientiousness or if you work on increasing your conscientiousness, since you are more likely to be dependable and follow through on your inner agreement. If you lack sufficient self-control to follow through, or if you are prone to cheating, personal rewards and penalties will be less effective.

I commonly have a slew of emails and related follow-ups and have trouble getting through them, since there are plenty of other things I would rather be doing. So I often establish an agreement with myself that I will get through fifty emails, for example, before I allow myself to eat lunch. Once I start getting hungry, I am even more motivated to get through them, and eventually the task is done. I always feel much better about getting the emails off of my plate, and I get my reward on my plate instead: lunch.

Mental Imagery

You can apply the "carrot and stick" principles of motivation to your own behaviors using positive and negative imagery. If you are doing things that you know you shouldn't, are not doing things that you know you should, or are simply stuck in a state of procrastination and inaction, applying what you know about avoidance and approach motivations is extremely helpful.

What you want to do in these instances is to get yourself to feel worse about that which you know you should not do and feel better about that which you know you should. Your emotions affect your rationality, and your rationality affects your emotions, so you are using rational thinking to purposefully influence your emotions.

Call up an image in your mind of you taking part in the behavior that you want to avoid. Now start imagining the negative outcomes associated with what is happening and what will happen if you continue down that path. Don't be vague in these mental images. You want to be as clear as possible so you invoke strong emotions within yourself. The images can be realistic ones, based on negative consequences that are actually happening; they can be images of what is likely to happen; or they can be completely fabricated. Your emotions don't know the difference unless your imagery is so ridiculous that your mind rejects the possibility entirely. And in the case of self-sabotaging behaviors, you probably don't need to fabricate any images at all, since there will be enough real negative images associated with them to you serve your purposes.

Use the same technique to motivate positive behaviors. Concentrate on the positive imagery associated with what you want to impel yourself to do. If you want to feel motivated to work out at the gym, for example, picture as vividly as you can how great you will feel afterwards, the time you'll be able to spend engaging actively with friends and family, the extra energy you will have, the personal satisfaction you will gain, and any other positive imagery you can generate. Think it through in detail, focusing entirely on positive mental images and emotions.

Mental Associations

Using mental associations is a similar technique to using mental imagery, except that you aren't so much conjuring up new images as you are building connections by establishing mental associations between existing factors in your life.

For example, let's say one of the most cherished aspects in your life is the fun you have spending time with your children. You know on a rational level that your current job has long hours and doesn't allow much time to do this, yet you seem unmotivated in taking the steps to look for more balanced employment. So, in your mind, you want to associate the actions around finding another job with the enjoyment of spending time with your kids, since this association increases your motivation to get on with looking for other employment.

I used this technique a fair bit when I was trying to overcome my apprehension about leaving my engineering job to pursue my current vocation. I had plenty of factors motivating me to stay put—and plenty of family and friends telling me not to quit my job as well. I used many of the motivating techniques we are covering, and one of the most effective for me was mental associations. I associated the aspects I enjoy in my life, such as freedom, family time, travel, self-direction, and opportunity, with the actions required for me to resign. I didn't even know if the associations I was focusing on were realistic at that point, but they helped tip the scales in terms of my motivation—which helped *make* them realistic.

Self-Talk and Affirmations

You can use self-talk in a similar way to mental imagery, out loud or in your mind. In fact, you almost certainly do already, though not necessarily helpfully.

The first step is to notice your existing self-talk surrounding your behaviors. It may be quite negative and self-degrading. If you tell yourself bad things about yourself all the time, it erodes your self-esteem and self-worth. But if you can focus your self-criticisms on behaviors you want to avoid, rather than attacking yourself overall, it does motivate you to find alternative behaviors.

Better still, use positive self-talk instead. Give yourself personal encouragement directed towards the behaviors or actions you want to adopt. In fact, try avoiding the negative altogether. You'll certainly feel better, especially if you're already prone to self-criticism. In a sense, in employing positive self-talk you are being your own cheerleader by mentally congratulating yourself and saying nice things about the behaviors you are shooting for. Combining self-talk with mental imagery makes the avoidance and approach motivations even stronger, and this is the approach I recommend.

Probably where I've used self-talk the most is near the end of running and biking races. When I feel like I can hardly push any further, I often say things to myself like "One more step!" "You're almost there!" or "You've got this!" to help me muster up additional motivation and energy.

Another way that you can use self-talk is through affirmations. Affirmations are positive words or sentences that you repeat either verbally or in your mind over and over again. The idea behind affirmations is that they influence the subconscious. Since the subconscious doesn't seem to differentiate past or future events from the present, affirmations should be repeated in the present tense. You might repeat "I am resilient" or "I am happy and healthy," for example.

The reasons why this works are the same reasons why hypnosis works. Hypnotists communicate with our subconscious minds when we are in a state of deep relaxation. We enter a hypnotic trance and become hyper-receptive to suggestion. Affirmations are really a form of self-hypnosis, and work particularly well when we are in a relaxed state of concentration. I have experienced positive results when I've repeated affirmation as part of the progressive muscle relaxation technique we will get to in the Summit of Self-Regulation.

Role Models

Personal development guru Jim Rohn has often been quoted as saying, "You're the average of the five people you spend the most time with." I'm not sure we can verify the scientific accuracy of this—or why it's five people in particular—but there is a lot of truth in its essence: we absorb many of the behaviors, attitudes, and actions of those that we spend time with.

What this means for you is: Surround yourself with people who are doing the things you admire. This primarily takes advantage of our affiliation motivation, but you are also influenced by perceived responses from role models—as well as by reciprocity. At the same time, watch out about spending significant time with negative people. Negative role models can drag us down and destroy us over time.

When we are children, our most important role models are generally our parents and caregivers, who have tremendous influence on us. As we grow older, we can choose our role models, and we need to choose wisely because they continue to influence our thoughts and actions throughout our lives.

Social Accountability

Social influence and reciprocity also come from your friends. But this doesn't mean that you need to have as many friends as possible—or Facebook "friends" or Twitter followers or other social media connections. What more and more studies are validating is that it isn't the quantity that matters, it is the quality. Quality relationships are built on fundamentals like trust, respect, acceptance, and understanding, as well as a willingness to invest time and energy. These are people who will run a hundred kilometers for you, and who you will run a hundred kilometers for. Possibly even literally.

A number of years ago, my sister-in-law and I decided to start a group challenge so we could hold each other accountable for getting out and running. That first year we called it "run or die July," and it was a challenge to run one hundred kilometers within the month.

We found a running app that allowed us to invite family and friends to join, as well as to track each other's progress, and on the first of July the running began. It was a ton of fun, and we spurred each other on to complete the challenge. We are now many years into organizing similar challenges amongst family and friends, and it is a tremendous motivator to get outside and to keep fit.

The accountability principal can also be applied more broadly. When you announce to the world or your larger peer group, for example, what your goals are, you feel a need to live up to your commitments. Accountability is one of the primary reasons why couples recite their wedding vows in front of family and friends. Nowadays, a lot of people announce their goals on social media for similar reasons. It helps them stay motivated along the journey.

There are a number of reasons why social accountability works. One is that you don't want to let people down that may be rooting for you and expose yourself to negative social judgment. A second reason is that you receive actual nudges and encouragement from other people that you may not even know. This happens all the time if you're using social media. And of course it makes use of reciprocity: the other person has given their time, focus, energy, and commitment to help you succeed, so you need to hold up your end of the agreement.

I've found accountability partners to be very beneficial in my life. Find someone who will encourage and hold you accountable for completing a certain activity by a deadline—ideally it's a reciprocal agreement where you also hold them accountable for whatever activity they are trying to work through, in which case a competitive aspect sometimes also plays a part. I have employed this strategy many times in motivating myself to finish creative endeavors, such as writing this book. For my writing, I have often promised certain sections to family members, coworkers, or friends, for example, by certain deadlines. I have also found others engaged in similar endeavors, and we've challenged each other to complete a certain number of words by a certain time.

Managing Your Motivations

Once you are fully committed to making positive changes, how do you stay motivated throughout the journey? If you're working through mental health challenges, staying motivated is easier said than done, since mental health challenges can, and often do, erode our motivations. In addition to applying the strategies we have just covered, I have found it helpful to maintain momentum by highlighting the small gains that I made—and I do mean small, because every progression can feel like taking two tiny steps up and then one step back down.

It's very similar to how acclimatization works in high-altitude mountaineering. The path forward is really a repeating up-and-back process: we make a push into the altitude, but then we have to go back down to allow our bodies to build red blood cells and adapt before we can push still farther up. When you are having these up-and-backs in your life, it is easy to dwell on the *back* parts, but that just pulls you back further. Congratulate yourself on each step. Don't dwell on what you haven't been able to improve yet, focus on what you have.

Above all, you have to take control of your own motivations. Otherwise, you end up being significantly, if not primarily, influenced and motivated by others who understand the motivating principles and use them to their advantage. This is especially true when it comes to susceptibility to media influence and advertising, since influencing people's motivations is essentially what the entire industry is built upon.

And you have to understand and not deny the role of your feelings. If you don't understand that it is your feelings that drive a lot of your decisions, you can more easily become victim to emotional appeals, such as people who appeal to the compassionate and caring motivations of people to scam them out of money under the guise of charity.

Take the time to understand and figure out ways of influencing your own motivations so that you are in control of which mountains you approach and how ambitiously you climb them.

Procrastination

The last thing I want to go into in a bit more detail on in this chapter is procrastination, since it leads into the next chapter. I am guilty of procrastinating more often than I would like, and it is something I'm continuously working on.

We might start with the question, "Why do I procrastinate?" This is the wrong question to ask. Procrastination is the norm; it is the default path, given that we would rather do things that we enjoy in the moment. It is a way we try to manage our mood because it feels better than having to work or take action.

A better question might be, "Why don't I procrastinate indefinitely?" The answer is usually because we have a panic alarm system that is wired into us. We're often stuck between doing an activity that we don't particularly want to do and experiencing a repercussion that we don't particularly want to experience. When we're not close to the deadline or the realization of the repercussions of inaction, we're not motivated enough to take action.

The problem with leaving things to the last minute is fairly obvious, although we usually don't appreciate it until it is too late. Activities are often more complex and take longer than we expect, so we run out of time, energy, or both. Also, we often have other priorities at the same time which compounds the problem. When we do get everything done in the end, it is at an extreme cost to our bodies and minds in the form of exhaustion, lack of sleep, anxiety, and mental fatigue. And while that is inevitable when scaling an actual high-altitude mountain, it is seldom necessary in our Summits of Self.

The path to the summit consists of many steps along the way, and this is where self-discipline comes into play, which we will be exploring further next, in the Summit of Self-Balance.

Expedition Debrief

Now it is your turn to determine what elements of self-motivation are helpful in influencing your own motivation towards moving your life forward. This is the real objective in exploring motivation. Your motivations are extremely complex, but even subtle changes in focus and thought patterns in small areas can manifest into the nudge you need to take action or continue moving.

What are your strongest intrinsic and extrinsic motivators, and how can you capitalize on these by reframing how you think about approaching your challenges and opportunities? Your personality distribution from the last chapter will give you some insight into this, as will observing your own behaviors and inclinations. Do you tend to rely more on your emotions or on rational thinking? Remember that both are critical to your decision-making and life experiences.

How will you apply some of the strategies we explored for motivating yourself? Mental imagery, mental associations, self-talk, and affirmations are strategies that you can apply in your own mind almost anywhere and at any time. I believe you will have the best success by combining these with the more external strategies of personal rewards, role models, and social accountably. Make use of the strategies and knowledge that help you increase your motivation towards meaningful change, and feel free to disregard the strategies that don't seem to resonate with you.

Motivation is what will get you to the point of taking the first steps needed in climbing your own mountains, so take your motivations seriously. Motivation will move you forward so that you can be proud of the mountains you've started climbing rather than regretting the mountains you wish you had attempted. Combined with the other strategies in this book, your self-motivation strategies are an essential part of your journey.

THE SUMMIT OF SELF-BALANCE

The Tour de Scottsdale

I learned a very important lesson in balance from biking, and it's not the lesson you might think.

When Natalie and I were living in Arizona, we signed up for a road-bike race known as the Tour de Scottsdale. It is a seventy-mile race that winds through the city before circumnavigating the McDowell Sonoran Preserve, with great mountain and valley views. The race takes place in the fall, which means that riders need to do their training during the scorching Arizona summers. In order to avoid riding during the heat of the day, when the temperatures would routinely soar to 115°F or higher, we would generally ride very early in the morning or very late at night. There were a few others from the engineering office who had also signed up for the race, so a number of times a week we would meet at around 5:00 a.m. to do a short ride before work.

For one of our training rides near the end of the summer, Natalie and I decided to bike the actual Tour de Scottsdale route on a Saturday morning. Since it was the weekend, we had slept in a bit later than we should have, and the sun was already cresting the horizon when we began the ride. The first few hours weren't too bad, but gradually the temperature became unbearable. We stopped at a convenience store at one point along the way to refill our water bottles, but we were having to drink almost continuously as well as pour water on our heads to try to cool our bodies.

During the last section of the ride, there was quite a long stretch without any stores or areas to stop to get additional water, and we both ended up running out. We tried pushing onward, since we knew there was a convenience store a few miles ahead, but within a few minutes we were getting dizzy and swerving back and forth on the road, unable to think clearly. We got off our bikes and stumbled over to a mesquite tree close to the side of the road to try to escape from the sweltering sun.

And then, suddenly, I started to hyperventilate. I collapsed on the ground and tried to consciously slow down my breathing, but I could do nothing: it was automatic and very rapid. My heart was pounding in my chest, and I was frightened at how I seemed to have no control over what was happening. And Natalie wasn't in much better shape. We were in trouble, and we tried frantically to figure out what we could possibly do about it. All I could think of was to wave my empty bottle in the air at passing vehicles in the hopes that someone might stop and offer us water.

One of the first few vehicles to pass by us was a pickup truck, and when the driver noticed us waving our water bottles, he pulled over and backed up along the curb to where we were sitting. He jumped out of his truck and asked if we were OK. To our great fortune, it turned out that he was a soldier in the US Army who had recently been posted in Iraq and was home visiting his mother. He was quite familiar with the symptoms of heat exhaustion and heatstroke; as he later explained to us, some of his troops had experienced similar problems. He immediately loaded us and our bikes in the back of his truck and drove us to his mother's house, which was in a gated community not far from where we had stopped. He brought us inside where it was air conditioned and gave us bananas and some electrolyte drinks.

We sat and spoke with him and his mother for quite a while before we thanked them sincerely for their kind hospitality and stood up with the intention of getting back on our bikes to continue riding back to where we had parked our jeep. I'm glad to say they talked us out of it, because I still wasn't thinking very clearly. We instead got back into the soldier's truck, and he drove us to our vehicle.

I thought the symptoms would subside once we were in the air conditioning of our jeep, but nausea kept building inside of me. When we got home, I took a shower right away to cool off, and I started vomiting almost as soon as I had turned the water on. I experienced a number of episodes of being sick to my stomach, as well as prolonged headaches, nausea, and generally feeling unsettled. I had to take two days off of work, and it was almost a week before the nausea fully subsided, my system was back in balance, and I started to feel normal again.

Having been raised in a relatively cold climate, I was quite familiar with the dangers of frostbite and hypothermia, as well as how to avoid them, but I had very little knowledge about the symptoms of heatstroke or the dangers associated with it. I know a lot more now.

What is interesting about heatstroke is that your internal temperature doesn't have to rise by much to put you in a very bad state. Your body normally maintains a temperature balance around 98.6°F and it only takes a few degrees, to around 104°F, for heatstroke to occur.

The Importance of Balance

Balance is perhaps the most important and foundational secret of existence. We see balance throughout the universe in many important ways. The Earth itself is essentially a giant buffer system that maintains a delicate balance to allow the existence of life as we know it, and though we usually take for granted phenomena like the Earth–atmosphere energy balance to regulate radiation from the sun and maintain a steady-state global climate, we're beginning to realize we shouldn't.

Our bodies are likewise delicate systems of balance where homeostasis is maintained through a series of complex, automatic sensory and control systems. There are many different properties that our bodies keep in balance, such as our internal temperature, glucose levels, acidity levels, blood pressure, hydration, and oxygen saturation. When any of these systems get too far out of balance, things go very badly for us. Although these systems are influenced indirectly by our conscious choices and actions, they are mostly controlled automatically. We should be thankful for these biologically automated systems, since it is challenging enough just trying to keep the rest of our lives in balance.

In addition to our automated systems, there are many conscious areas of our lives where balance is important as well, and those are what we're going to focus on in this chapter. As with our automatic systems, when we make conscious decisions that take us too far from equilibrium, we start to experience problems—physically, mentally, spiritually, emotionally, or in some combination.

At the base of all of this, of course, is the bottom level of Maslow's pyramid: physical needs. Just as you can't look after higher-level motivations unless your basic needs are taken care of, you can't maintain psychological balance without your physical systems being in balance—as I discovered in my bicycling misadventure. Our physical well-being depends on a well-balanced approach to nourishment and proper exercise. Most of us seem to know and understand this on a conscious level, but we don't always put it into practice. I'm lucky: I learned and inherited a good physical balance from my father. He modeled good lifestyle choices for me, and his genes passed on to me a body type that's easier to keep in shape. Not everyone has this kind of advantage, and some people have to work harder than others to stay in shape. This is why it is key to understand our individual metabolisms, habits, and challenges.

Basic interpersonal balance is also essential, and family is at the core of that. If we do not have a functioning family life—if, for instance, we are estranged from our family, either by choice, misfortune, or by lack of effort—our lives are out of balance. We all live very busy lives, but it is important to consciously and deliberately schedule significant family time, both with our immediate and extended family, or loyal friends in the case of those without family, lest we develop far-reaching structural and functional severances to familial bonds.

Now that I have three kids of my own, I give a fair bit of thought to the balance of influence I should have in my children's lives and decisions. There is an argument to be made for unconditional acceptance and being OK with whatever path children want to take, but there is also an argument to be made for encouragement and discipline to keep children on the path you believe is best for them. Children differ in their temperaments and in many other important areas, so a one-size-fits-all approach doesn't exist. But it is fair to say that here, too, balance is better than extremes.

Relationships with friends also require balance. The best balance between social and personal time for you is highly predicated on your level of extraversion, so you need to discover it and maintain it on an individual level. Learn to recognize the indicators that you may not have the balance right: if you feel overwhelmed and irritated by others, it can be a simple indicator that you may need more alone time; if you feel lonely or bored, it's often an indicator of the need for more social interaction. To some of us this may seem obvious, but we're not always honest with ourselves because of what we think is expected of us. Pay attention to your emotions: they are an excellent feedback mechanism for finding your social balance.

And there is your bank balance. Finding the right balance between saving and spending is really Personal Finance 101, but not everyone is equally good at it. Excessive spending catches up with us eventually, and excessive debt is not healthy; on the other side of the balance sheet, it isn't particularly healthy to prioritize saving over all else. I know people who have done that at the expense of quality experiences with their children, for example. If your finances are out of balance in either direction, it will affect your psychological health overall.

Naturally, the bank balance is an easier question if you have more money, which you may get by working more. And it is good to work—but not all the time. Do you work to live or live to work? You need to work not only to survive but also to live a fruitful and balanced life. Pay attention to your emotions: workaholics are motivated by negative emotions like anxiety, guilt, irritation, and personal disappointment, whereas individuals pursuing work for engagement and fulfillment are motivated by the joy their work brings, self-improvement, enthusiasm, and excitement. I have noticed my own tendencies towards workaholism, and I have to frequently make adjustments to counter them.

Balance is even important when it comes to your philanthropic focus and activities. Concern for self and concern for others are very much connected, as we've already been exploring, but just as it is possible to be so self-absorbed that you overlook others, it is also possible to be so concerned with the well-being of others that you neglect yourself. Neither is healthy.

One of the most challenging yet eye-opening things for us to do as humans is to truly consider ideas and viewpoints that are contrary to our own. As we've seen in the Summit of Self-Knowledge, when we adopt a particular stance on something, we often set up a perimeter of reason that we use to filter and distort other viewpoints so that we can bolster our own conclusions. Our ideas and viewpoints become a part of us, and when they are challenged, it feels like an assault on our beings, not just our ideas.

It is healthy to have a stance on issues, and an important step in assuming a productive role in society, but we have to realize that we aren't always right. In fact, if we're honest with ourselves, we end up being wrong a fair bit. If we want to continue to grow and to discover new truths in life, we have to be willing to put our egos aside and give alternative viewpoints a deep consideration. This is how we help to iron out implicit biases and broaden our own relatively narrow avenues of thought.

Political views are particularly polarizing, and the customization of news content via social media channels has exacerbated this. When it comes to complex debates, often both sides are partially correct and the best solutions are usually arrived at through careful deliberation and balancing of alternative viewpoints. We have many multifaceted socioeconomic challenges to work through that simply cannot be solved with a one-sided ideology. We need to talk things through, which also means listening and not silencing others or refusing to engage in civil discourse. The path to successful outcomes is through constructive dialogue; wearing blinders commits to not only imbalance but disaster.

Of course you probably have strong opinions on many important topics, but if you really want to broaden your own outlook and even understand your own position better, put yourself in the shoes of your antagonist and really try to think of things from the other perspective. This includes balancing the media sources you consume as well. This may be uncomfortable, but it's necessary for both balance and growth.

And, along with balance in how you respond to and treat others, you need balance in how you respond to and treat yourself: the psychological balance between self-acceptance and self-discipline. This balance spans and influences all of the areas of life-balance we can conceive of.

Self-Acceptance

Self-acceptance is exactly what the term implies: it is the degree to which we accept ourselves as we are, with all of our strengths, weaknesses, deficiencies, and choices. It is one of the most important aspects affecting our mental health. When I think of someone in my life who seemed to embody self-acceptance, my grandmother comes to mind. She and my grandfather were the two sides of this psychological balance: he was very self-disciplined, while she was very self-accepting. She always looked for the positive despite the life of challenges and hardships she had led. She contracted polio when she was in her late twenties, pregnant, and had a two-year-old and four-year-old at home to look after. She was in the hospital for four months and was left with mild paralysis for the rest of her life. This significantly affected her mobility, but she didn't allow it to get in the way of raising a large family and living out a good life.

I remember her telling me about her journey with religion. As part of her growth and desire to break free of the social restraints of her generation, at one point in her life she decided to attend services in as many religions as she could. She wanted to gain a better appreciation of the overarching principals that connected all religions, and she didn't allow such exploration to be swayed by external influence or condemnation. Her deep sense of self-acceptance also led to a generous acceptance of other people on their own path, a characteristic I much admired.

When I was struggling with GAD, it was not until I was finally able to learn to accept and love that part of me at the deepest level that it started to melt away. As much as I hated that knot of uncomfortable tension within me, I had to remind myself that it was a part of me and not something foreign. And that is a difficult point to get to: to learn to love a part of yourself that you've grown to detest. Telling yourself that you love that part of you is confusing and frustrating. Your subconscious mind doesn't believe it. But self-acceptance is about putting down the weapons that we use against ourselves and stopping the fight. It is the fighting and internal resentment that is perpetuating the problems.

It is a bit like climbers trying to fight against the effects of lower oxygen availability at altitude. Trying to push harder or frantically force yourself to move quicker is ultimately self-defeating. On Everest, I had a few times where I pushed too hard and then collapsed on the snow; one time, I even temporarily lost my vision as my gasping lungs attempted to bring me back to awareness. It is through accepting the reality of oxygen deprivation and working within such constraints that climbers are able to inch their way forward and remain conscious, one tiny step at a time. And it is through accepting the reality of who you are right now that you can see how to move forward from it.

The next step beyond acceptance is gratitude. In the Summit of Self-Motivation, we looked at the effects of positively programming your mind with affirmations and positive imagery; gratitude is also part of that. Findings have shown that feeling grateful for what you have is beneficial for both physical and mental health as well as overall happiness. Because we have finite concentration capabilities, thoughts of gratitude shift our minds away from negative thoughts, such as jealousy and resentment, allowing us to experience more positive emotion.

Gratitude for what you have can also aid your self-acceptance. Try taking some time each day to think of or list the things that you are grateful for. Journaling can be a good tool for this—as long as you're writing down what you're thankful for, not your complaints for the day.

And there is also a tremendous amount of benefit in being grateful to others. Thank the people around you for their support and influence. It needs to be genuine appreciation, which tends to create an atmosphere of positivity. Gratefulness to others is extremely positive and inspiring for them, which naturally improves your social bonds, but even in itself it has an immensely positive impact on you: it tells you that you have people in your life to be thankful for, and it tells you that you are the kind of person who is good to others. It is a habit that needs to be cultivated, but it is worth the effort.

Forgiveness is a related aspect of self-acceptance. It isn't uncommon for people to say to themselves "I'll never forgive myself!" after they've made a mistake. We may be saying it tongue-in-cheek, but often we do hold onto internal condemnation for a long time, and it burns negativity into us like holding onto a hot iron instead of releasing it. Learn from your mistakes, but keep the past in the past.

This is also why we need to forgive others. When others do us wrong, it isn't that they necessarily *deserve* forgiveness, though they may. But *we* don't deserve to carry the resentment around with us like a heavy burden for the rest of our lives. It becomes like a disease that devours us slowly from the inside. Forgiving others can help free us from the continual suffering and negative effects that holding onto wrongdoings has on our own lives.

Take a few minutes to think about some of the grudges that you have been holding onto and need to let go. It probably won't take you long to identify them. As much as you think you don't want to let such grudges go, realize that it really is in your own best interest to do so. You will feel a weight lifted from your shoulders when you can release them.

Self-Discipline

The area just above Base Camp on the southern route up Everest is known as the Khumbu Icefall. It is a treacherous section made of thousands of enormous blocks of ice, called seracs, and many crevasses in the ice that are often hundreds of feet deep and must be crossed by aluminum ladders tied end to end. And it's moving: the Khumbu Glacier moves at four to six feet (between one and two meters) per day, and it creates the icefall as it breaks off and cascades down the steep slope towards Base Camp. Most climbers consider the icefall the most dangerous section of the southern route up Everest, and many climbers have been killed by falling seracs or ice avalanches in it. The majority of the ice movement each day happens once the sun hits the ice and the ice begins to expand, so, in order to mitigate the risk, climbers often try to get through the icefall very early in the morning.

When my family was climbing Everest, we had to go through the Khumbu Icefall six times as part of our acclimatization

strategy, returning to Base Camp after each climb into the altitude. We knew the importance of getting through as much of the
icefall as we could before sunrise, so we would set our alarms for
around 2:00 a.m. in order to get an early start. When my alarm
would go off, the last thing I really wanted to do was to get out
of my warm sleeping bag in the dead of night and start preparing
for an arduous, more than eight-hour climb. But I had to force
myself to do it if I was going to continue to the summit.

We have already mapped the route to the Summit of Self-
Motivation, but emotional motivation can only take us so far if
we want to live a purposeful life. A discovery that I made fairly
early on about success in life is that unsuccessful people and successful people both have many things that they don't want to do.
The difference is that successful people do them anyways. This
is the essence of self-discipline.

My grandfather was a beacon of self-discipline in my life, the
opposite side of the balance from my self-accepting grandmother.
He lived through the Great Depression and, like many in his
generation, he retained many of the disciplined tendencies that
were imperative during those years. I learned much of my self-
discipline from observing and emulating him—though not all
of it was healthy. He had his own weight management regimen,
for example. He would weigh himself every morning to keep
track. When he determined he had become overweight by his
standards, he would stop eating until he was again satisfied with
his weight. Similarly, when his weight would drop below what he
had determined to be optimal, he would enjoy hefty meals and
even buffets. I'm sure most nutritionists would not approve, but
he maintained his optimal weight throughout his life.

I have said a lot about the importance of self-acceptance and
self-love, and at first self-discipline may appear inconsistent
with that. But if we love ourselves, we have to help ourselves
grow. There is a quote I like from Nkosiphambili Molapis: "The
'good life' begins when you stop wanting a better one." From a
contentment perspective, I think this valid—but it is really only

half true when we look at our lives overall: we need to continuously improve if we want to live meaningful lives and not lapse into complacency and self-neglect. We have to balance our self-acceptance with self-discipline so that we can recognize and correct the aspects of us that need improvement.

In many ways, we need to learn to treat ourselves as we would a close friend that we care about deeply and want to succeed. We wouldn't—or at least shouldn't—coddle a close friend to the point of enabling them to perpetuate actions or thoughts that cause them long-term distress. Giving them a firm nudge when needed—"tough love"—has the sufferer's best interests in mind. And yet on the other hand we wouldn't—or at least shouldn't—be too hard on someone we love and care about. We don't want them to suffer any unnecessary pain, so we are gentle and caring in our actions and recommendations.

How Self-Disciplined Can You Be?

We often refer to self-discipline as willpower or self-control. It is the ability to override our emotional motivation and do what we think makes logical sense, rather than what we may feel like doing at the time. But it's not as simple as just deciding to be more self-disciplined. For one thing, self-discipline comes easier to those who are higher in the personality trait of conscientiousness. And for another, self-discipline is a limited resource for all of us—although it does get replenished over time. Social psychologist Roy Baumeister and his colleagues discovered this phenomenon, referred to as ego depletion. If we are continuously having to resist temptations over and over again, we eventually run out of resolve.

You have probably experienced this in your own life many times. It is a cycle that seems to repeat over and over again for many people—for instance, people who diet to manage their weight. With most new diets, there are certain foods that the weight-watcher must avoid, and people tend to have a degree of self-discipline to resist the temptation for the first few days. Then a week or two passes and it seems harder and harder to resist those sweet and savory favorite treats. Then a large extended-family dinner comes up and the self-discipline pillar crumbles entirely. "I'll start dieting again next week!" takes over.

When your self-discipline eventually fails, what has happened psychologically is that your rational decisions have been over-thrown and displaced by your emotional motivations, which sometimes include your desire to do nothing. Brain analysis has shown that when individuals have run out of self-discipline, they have lower blood-glucose levels and brain activity is decreased in the frontal cortex, where logical reasoning takes place.

Self-discipline is important for all of us, but I think it is par-ticularly important for self-employed individuals. When I used to work for a large company, I had a fair number of external motiva-tors in the form of managers and bosses, along with more subtle peer motivations and collaborative efforts to keep everyone mov-ing forward. Once I became self-employed, I didn't have those anymore.

Self-discipline can produce immediate observable results—such as losing weight quickly or being able to climb Everest. But there is often quite a disconnect between effort and outcome, and then it is tempting, and easy, to fall into complacency. Much of what I do in marketing and networking, for example, does not have any business outcome in the end, and the small percentage that does often takes significant time to come to fruition. Since I never know at the time what is going to work and what isn't, I've learned to be self-disciplined in doing the work anyways. I have to live with delayed gratification.

This is one of the most significant behavioral differences between successful individuals and unsuccessful individuals, no matter what domain we identify for success: the ability to resist immediate rewards in order to reap greater future rewards. Delayed gratification has deep evolutionary roots. Among our distant ancestors, those that learned to store food and resources for future hard times were the ones that ultimately survived, so natural selection has rewarded the human ability to delay gratification.

When I finished high school, many of my classmates rushed out and bought trucks, motorcycles, and similar things for themselves as soon as they started working and had a few dollars. I wanted to do the same, and I felt a bit jealous. It wasn't particularly gratifying saving up my money to put it towards my education—but I could see the rewards at the far end of that journey. I could have borrowed money, but debt limits our freedom to make changes in our lives, especially career changes. It's like the nervous coworker I mentioned in the Summit of Self-Motivation, who was so in debt he couldn't afford to lose his job. We become overly reliant on our employers, and we're often unable to even consider other options for fear of losing the steady income the we've become reliant on. In essence, we exchange freedom for security.

And so, when I started working as an engineer after university, I opted to minimize any debts and avoid them altogether when I could. For the first few years, I rented rooms in other people's houses or stayed in inexpensive bed-and-breakfasts nearby the office. There were a number of times when I couldn't find an available room so I slept in the back of my car—including two times in the dead of winter, which wasn't very pleasant to say the least! But the upside of this delayed gratification was that by the time Natalie and I bought our first house, we bought it entirely with money we had been saving and investing. We didn't have a mortgage, car payments, or other liabilities. We lived debt free, and that gave us a huge amount of freedom.

Henry Ford is often credited with a quote that hits on an important aspect of self-discipline: "Whether you think you can, or you think you can't, you're right." Our beliefs and attitudes towards our own willpower are an important factor in our ability to resist temptation and delay gratification. Researcher Veronika Job and her colleagues made this discovery, which upended a lot of the traditional thinking about how self-discipline works. People who believe that their own willpower is easily exhaustible show more signs of depletion than when their beliefs are manipulated to believe it is not easily exhaustible.

Which means that if you really want to be more self-disciplined, you need to believe in your own capacity to be self-disciplined. This may be easier said than done, but many of the techniques and insights in this book can help you challenge and alter your thinking in order to bolster such beliefs, little by little.

Time Blocking

Can you use specific techniques to improve your self-discipline? Of course. Time blocking is one. It's a strategy whereby you schedule blocks of time throughout the day for specific activities and stick to your schedule, only allowing yourself to focus on those specific activities. I use time blocking extensively in my business and personal life. I don't usually schedule my entire day, but when I have particular activities that I don't feel like doing or just haven't been getting to, I block off periods of time, usually in one- or two-hour blocks, and only allow myself to work on those particular activities during that time. I used the time blocking strategy extensively when writing this book, for example. I set a timer and only allowed myself to work on writing and editing during that time. When emails popped up on my computer and other distractions arose, I ignored them until I was through the time period I had blocked off.

When I do this, at first it doesn't feel like I'm being very productive. There are often other things I would rather be doing, so I'm sluggish to start. But since I'm not allowing myself to be pulled away to the other things my mind is trying to distract me with, I eventually get in the groove and gain momentum. Often, by the time I am finished my time block, I'm on such a roll that the time has flown by and I've made huge progress.

Time blocking helps keep us focused, first and foremost, but it also helps preserve mental energy. It takes time and mental energy every time we have to reorient ourselves to a different activity. We like to think that we are being effective by "multi-tasking," but decades of research has shown us that switching our attention back and forth between tasks, or trying to do multiple tasks simultaneously, significantly reduces our productivity and memory, and can reduce our cognitive ability. Even as early as 1931, psychologist Charles Telford identified the psychological refractory period, the time between two successive tasks where our response to the second stimulus is delayed because we are still processing the first. And no, you're not doing both things at the same time. The term multitasking is a misnomer: our brains don't do more than one thing at a time, so we're switching back and forth between tasks at the expense of effectiveness. Neuroscientists David Strayer and Jason Watson found that only 2.5 percent of people can truly multitask effectively—a subset of the population that they refer to as *supertaskers*. If you think you're one of them, the odds are that you're kidding yourself. You may like feeling busy, but you need to remind yourself that activity is not necessarily accomplishment. Busyness isn't the goal; effectiveness is.

Pause to Regain Balance

Now that we've explored the two sides of the psychological self-balance continuum—self-acceptance and self-discipline—the challenge is finding what balance is right within your life. This balance is something that only you can decide, and it involves paying attention to your inner feedback, your average stress levels, your personal productivity, and even the comments from those you know and trust. Others may have noticed aspects of your self-balance that you have missed, so it is worth listening with an open mind. There is a time for productive and disciplined work and there is a time for just letting things be as they are.

Another major reason why finding the right balance is so important in our personal and professional lives is because of the way stress is related to performance. The Yerkes-Dodson Law, which was developed in 1908 by psychologists Robert Yerkes and John Dodson, does a good job of depicting the relationship between stress arousal and performance. It is a parabolic relationship: when our stress levels are very low, our performance is low, and when our stress levels are very high, our performance is low as well. In other words, our performance increases as our mental and physiological state of arousal increases, but only to a certain point, after which further stress arousal actually decreases our performance. Optimum performance comes at moderate stress levels.

HEBBIAN VERSION OF THE YERKES-DODSON LAW

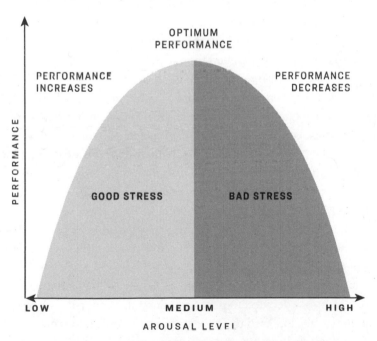

* Some anxiety can help with focus and attention

Adapted from R.M. Yerkes, J.D. Dodson, and D.O. Hebb

This may seem somewhat counterintuitive, but I'm sure you have noticed the truth of this in your own life. The times when you have been able to perform best are not when you are feeling completely relaxed and not when you are feeling completely stressed-out either.

High stress in particular is also very detrimental to innovation. When our stress levels are high, it is harder to think outside the box because we go into production mode rather than creative mode. Our motor function increases, as it does when we sense any threat, but our perception, creativity, and overall effectiveness are hindered. For assembly lines and industries that rely primarily on replication speed of preplanned procedures, this can have benefit, but most industries nowadays are part of the knowledge economy, where innovation and creativity is a must in order to stay relevant and competitive. You can't do groundbreaking work if you're constantly in crisis mode.

And sometimes you just need to pause. A pause is an opportunity to reflect and evaluate what is working and what is not. It is a time to determine if we need to make changes in our life-balance and which direction we need to move the needle.

Interestingly enough, our most creative times in life are often when we are taking a pause. We're able to look at our lives—our professions, our families, and other aspects—from an elevated perspective, without being so involved in what we are doing that it obscures our creativity.

Sometimes we are more or less forced into taking a pause in life by a lay-off, an economic downturn, or a family emergency. Although these times are troubling, they can also be the catalyst that we need in order to take a breath, reevaluate, and refocus. Take an enforced pause as a gift.

Not everyone wants to, of course. One year for Christmas my brother-in-law decided to play a prank on my father-in-law by giving him a fake gift card to a spa experience. After unwrapping the gift, my father-in-law stared for a minute at the gift card with his mouth open in disbelief. He was a lifelong farmer who seldom even let a doctor examine him, and there was no way he would let a masseuse anywhere near. As we all broke out laughing, we could see he was struggling with how to graciously accept such a gift without insulting the giver. My brother-in-law didn't let him squirm for too long, though, before he explained it was just a joke and brought out another gift he had hidden away earlier.

I used to think I would be uncomfortable—or perhaps even bored—at a spa, mainly because I always liked to keep busy. One winter a few years back, however, my parents decided to take us all to a Scandinavian spa. There had been heavy snowfall during the night and it was still coming down as we drove up to the entrance, laying a thick blanket of snow all over the property except for in the narrow pathways that had been shoveled. We each had a therapeutic massage before heading out to the spas, where we spent a good part of the day moving between hot pools, cold plunges, steam rooms, infusion rooms, and different styles of saunas. There was even a float pool underneath one of the buildings that was a high-salt bath in a quiet room, with gentle music that was broadcast through the water only. The ambience was serene, and I began to realize the benefits of integrating this type of relaxation and rejuvenation into our lives.

I'm not saying that a spa experience is necessarily the answer for you, but I am saying take a look at your own life and the degree to which you prioritize busyness and accomplishments over taking time to recharge. If your life is off balance and you are stuck in a pattern of perpetual striving, it may be worth exploring a few ways to pause to regain balance.

Expedition Debrief

Do you feel like you have a good balance between self-acceptance and self-discipline? It is important to develop your abilities to exercise both sides of the spectrum, because at times in your life you will sway too far to one side or the other and need to steer yourself back on course. Remember that the same principles of balance that keep the universe and our planet working are important in all areas of your life. Neglecting one or more areas is a recipe for disruption and trouble in other areas as well.

We didn't focus too heavily on self-acceptance strategies in this chapter because we'll be covering many of the mindfulness exercises in the next chapter, but rejuvenation, gratitude, and forgiveness are all important pieces of the self-acceptance puzzle. Being cognizant of practicing and expressing these qualities daily makes a huge difference. What do you have to be thankful for right now, and are you harboring resentment towards yourself or others that you need to release?

Self-discipline is your rational counterpart to the motivations we explored in the last chapter. What should you be doing that you are not doing, and what are you doing that you shouldn't? You know what these actions are, and self-discipline is what will get you there. Remember that self-discipline behaves like a limited asset that is depleted the more we have to use it and rely on it, so take steps in ensuring you start with a full tank and aren't frivolously exhausting your resources on things that aren't part of the mountains you know you should be climbing. The time blocking strategies can help your self-discipline, but the key is to find what works for you. Your beliefs about your own willpower are also critical factors, so refer back to the Summit of Self-Knowledge for ideas on challenging and altering limiting beliefs you may hold.

Lastly, do you take time to pause and recalibrate? Resting and allowing your body to acclimatize is a necessary part of any climb. In the busy, fast-paced society we live in, taking a pause can help you gain clarity, see the big picture, and recover the balance you need for optimal living.

SUMMIT FOUR

THE SUMMIT OF SELF-REGULATION

Swimming with the Manta Rays

One year, before we had kids, my wife and I went on vacation for a week to Hawaii. As part of the trip, we booked two nights at the Sheraton near Kona on the Big Island.

It was late in the evening when we checked in. We wandered down to a patio overlooking the ocean and saw people in the water: a long trail of snorkelers bobbing up and down, holding onto a series of floating pool noodles tied together, all illuminated by spotlights. At night, we learned, the hotel shines bright spotlights into the ocean in front of one of the hotel restaurants to attract plankton to the area, which in turn entices giant manta rays to come close to the rocky shoreline to feed. Manta rays are fascinating sea creatures that have underwater wings spanning up to eighteen feet from one tip to the other. There are many local snorkeling companies that take tourists there in boats at night to see the manta rays swooping through the water below them.

My wife and I aren't fans of controlled tours where tourists are corralled and directed in lines like cattle—it takes away from the natural and spontaneous excitement and wonder. But we were intrigued by the prospect of snorkeling with manta rays. So the next day, on an excursion into the nearby small city of Kailua-Kona, we happened on a dive shop, so we went in and asked about options to see the manta rays. They recommended we take a tour; we explained that we weren't crazy about organized tours and asked if we might be able to explore on our own, since we had brought our own masks and snorkels on the trip. They recommended against this because of the difficulty and potential danger involved in clambering down the rocky cliffs, but they said it was up to us and they could rent us waterproof dive flashlights if we liked. That sounded like a great idea to me.

Early that evening, while it was still light out, we went for a walk along the jagged lava-rock shoreline to scope out a place that would be less treacherous to enter the ocean. After some distance we found a secluded area where the lava rock was not quite as cliff-like and we could clamber down to the water's edge without too much difficulty. It was a ways from the location of the manta rays, though—not even within sight. Nevertheless, once the sun was down, we changed into our bathing suits; grabbed our masks, snorkels, and rented dive lights; and walked down towards this secluded location.

It is one thing wandering along a shoreline in the light of day, but it is a whole different experience in the pitch dark. With our dive lights, we were eventually able to find our way back to the spot, but the location felt very different. There was no light at all except for the narrow beams of our dive lights, and the splash of the surf against the lava rock made a hollow and eerie noise in the thick silence all around us.

Thinking about slipping into the dark water at that time of night was a bit anxiety-inducing, to say the least. I was picturing the shark from the movie *Jaws* lurking out there somewhere in the darkness. I could tell that Natalie wasn't any keener than I was to lower ourselves off of the lava rock into the unknown. It didn't take much for us to convince each other that we should go back to the front of the hotel where the spotlights were. We walked back and started climbing down the rocks in front of the hotel, but without the protection of the bay, the waves were crashing against the rocks and the surge of the ocean was rushing up and down the rock faces, creating whirlpools and small waterfalls every time it retreated. I've been in similar ocean surges, and they are fairly dangerous, even in the daylight, as the surge can quickly throw you against a rock and knock you unconscious. We decided it was too risky there. Our only option to enter the water would be the secluded area back along the edge of the bay. But my heart was still thumping in my chest at the thought of entering the dark waters.

Why were we so fearful of entering the water by ourselves in the pitch dark? Was there really any more risk of being attacked by a shark there rather than in the spotlights of the hotel where the tourist boats were anchored? I've learned to watch out for whether I'm avoiding a situation due to anxieties and phobias rather than real dangers. Avoidance behavior can be self-reinforcing, as I've already talked about in my own personal story. Now, there *is* an increased risk of shark attacks at night due to their feeding behaviors, but I knew that the odds of dying in a car crash driving around the island that day were far higher than the odds of being attacked by a shark that evening. I didn't want to make the common mistake of letting my mind overemphasize a risk just because of its dramatic nature. This is the essence of an irrational fear—where the magnitude of the fear is inflated beyond what is considered rational.

But I was still petrified at the thought of entering the dark, unknown waters. And I could tell that Natalie was having the same thoughts. We talked it over. In the end we decided that we couldn't let fear get the better of us, and back through the darkness we trudged towards the lava-rock entry point.

With our hearts beating rapidly, we made our way to the water's edge and put on our masks. The night seemed even darker at that point, with a thick mist all around us. There was still a decent amount of surge, and the noise of the waves against the rock in the otherwise heavy silence added to our uneasiness. I decided not to waste any additional time second guessing myself. I watched the waves for a short while so I could best time the swell and lowered myself backward into the dark water when the surge was high. My heart was racing, and I was treading water rapidly, trying to stay a few feet away from the rocks so I wouldn't be knocked against them. Natalie followed in the same way shortly after, and we started swimming out from shore to make our way around the point to where the manta rays would hopefully be. There were a number of small rocky outcroppings that we had to navigate around with our dive lights, and we held hands tightly as we swam together, neither of us wanting to let the other out of reach.

The ocean was definitely still alive at night. There were a lot of slender, needle-like fish about the length of our forearms that circled around us right near the surface. Every so often one of them would brush up against Natalie's face and she would recoil, squeezing my hand tightly and causing me to twist around with my dive light, trying to spot whatever creature in the darkness had caused her to lurch.

Eventually, after ten or fifteen minutes of swimming through the darkness, we made our way around the point. There was a tourist boat that had arrived, which made us feel less vulnerable. Before long, we were in the floodlit area.

Two manta rays, the larger one having roughly an eight-foot wingspan, had just arrived at the location to get their nightly feed of plankton. We dove down to get a close look at the magnificent creatures as they swooped and twisted above our heads and all around us. At times it would seem like they were going to run headlong into us, but then they would gracefully turn at the last moment. It was a wonderful experience, being so up close and personal with them. We stayed for an hour or so swimming with the rays before we decided we should head back.

The return swim wasn't quite as nervewracking, although it was not that easy to find the place where we had entered, since all the black lava rock looked nearly the same. And there were sea urchins all over the rocks beneath the water's edge, their black spines sticking out in every direction. I waited for a large swell and hoisted myself up onto the rocks, but Natalie didn't have quite the same success. She was partway out of the water when the swell she was relying on receded and she fell back in, landing right on top of a large sea urchin and getting a number of the black spines stuck in her backside. Once she was out of the water, we pulled them out right away.

We were ecstatic! We hugged each other and were like giddy school kids as we pranced back towards the hotel to change into dry clothes. We had faced our fears and transcended them, and we felt terrific about it. We went out for a late dinner at a nearby restaurant. As we sat out on their patio, high on a hill overlooking the water, the waitress came up to our table and said, "OK, you guys have to tell me where you just came from, because I can tell you're on a high right now!"

We were. That was a great experience and a great night.

Emotional Maturity

I've had other experiences as well where I've been courageous enough to face my irrational fears head-on and transcend them. But I've also had times when I've been too cowardly or timid to do so, and it's left me with a feeling of failure and eroded my self-worth. Luckily, the erosion is reversible: we can use our failures as learning experiences and make commitments to ourselves about how we will behave differently in future. It comes down to learning *emotional self-regulation*, which is the summit we are ascending in this chapter.

Emotional self-regulation is our ability to use our rational minds to influence and manage our emotions—which emotions we have, our degree or intensity of emotional arousal, how our emotions are expressed or manifested in our behaviors, and how often and for how long we experience an emotion. It's what we often call emotional maturity. It's one of the most important areas we can focus on if we want to minimize periods of suffering and maximize periods of joy and fulfillment in our lives.

Probably the most problematic aspect of low emotional maturity is that out-of-control emotions suppress rational thinking. When we feel we are in a crisis, our brain goes into survival mode, which allows sensory information to bypass our neocortex—the rational thinking part of our brain—and be processed directly by our amygdala—the emotional part of our brain. This is what is known as *amygdala hijacking*, a term coined by Daniel Goleman. Amygdala hijacking allows us to react quickly, but such reactions take place with little or no thinking, so they are generally irrational or overblown. If someone is prone to this, their lack of reflection and forethought makes them highly susceptible to blindly supporting emotionally charged notions and ideologies. Unfortunately, we can see examples of this being acted out in real time everywhere and often. And when people act without thinking, we pay the price as a society in the long run.

For this chapter, we'll mostly be exploring cognitive strategies for internal changes that we can make to influence and regulate our emotions. I should be clear, however, that making external changes is often just as important. Sometimes our external environments are so stressful and chaotic that strategies for self-regulation seem like tossing a pail of water on a forest fire. It is important to look at whether you need to make structural changes in your life as well—simplifying your life, reducing liabilities, decluttering, or even changing jobs. We will look more at this in the Summit of Self-Actualization.

The Rapids

In my last years of university and the first several years when I started working as an engineer, my friend George and I would travel with our kayaks up to the white-water region of the Ottawa River a couple of times a year. The Ottawa River has some world-class rapids, and both George and I had short "play boats" designed for white-water kayaking that were about six feet (just under two meters) long and allowed us to surf the standing waves and have lots of fun plunging and spinning in the rough water.

In white-water kayaking, we wear a neoprene skirt that seals the opening of the kayak so that it is watertight and maintains buoyancy even when flipped upside down. The most important maneuver for kayakers to know is a kayak roll, which allows you to right yourself quickly when flipped upside down, without having to eject from the kayak. Performing this maneuver on a calm lake is tricky enough, but it's particularly challenging when there is surging water and currents all around you and you don't really know your orientation to begin with. If you are unable to flip yourself upright, there is also a loop on the front of the neoprene skirt that allows you to break the watertight seal while upside down and eject from the kayak as an emergency backup maneuver. I had become quite proficient at performing the roll in various conditions, so I almost never had to eject; I would just roll back upright over and over again as I played in the surging water.

One year, all the rivers and lakes in the area were uncharacteristically flooded from the spring melt, so the Ottawa River had some of the highest water levels and largest hydraulic features on record. George and I decided we should check out what all the extra water had created.

The river looked completely different. Many of the typical features were nonexistent because they were so far underwater, but new giant waves and holes had been created. There is one enormous wave that only emerges in very high water called Bus Eater, for example—a name given to it because the cavity before the wave is deep enough to engulf a bus.

We were partway down the river when we finally arrived at the Coliseum Rapid, one of the largest rapids even under normal conditions. We got out of our kayaks before going through to scout the rapid and plan our route. The first standing wave on that rapid has been given the name White Faced Monster: it's a huge wave that looks like a wall of water with a recirculating hole in front of it and a little to one side. That particular year it was massive. We knew to avoid the recirculating hole because kayakers and rafters have often gotten stuck in it for significant periods of time as the recirculating water tosses them around and around. Most are thrown out of the hole eventually and live to tell the tale, but it is wise to avoid that area.

Once we had chosen our route, we got back into our kayaks and pushed off from shore. My heart was already racing; as I approached the rapid, the roar of the water was menacing.

I had been through big water features before and knew the technique. It is best to raise your paddle high above your head just before you hit the wave, since your kayak and body are plunged underwater but the top of the wave pushes up on the raised paddle and lifts you and your kayak back up. This position also provides some stability and the ability to make rapid movements to counter lateral currents. The surging water in large standing waves is highly turbulent and unpredictable, so you have to be ready for anything.

When I hit the wave, a surge of water, combined with the buoyancy of my kayak resurfacing, flung me into the air, and I landed upside down in the raging water on the back side of the wave. I tried to roll back upright but couldn't—I didn't know which way was up. I tried rolling three more times but was not even able to even get a gasp of air, so I had to pull the loop and eject from my kayak.

Once I was free from my boat, the buoyancy of my paddle jacket brought me to the surface, and I was able to get a quick gasp of air into my lungs before I was pulled underwater again. There were many slightly smaller waves and hydraulic features downstream from the White Faced Monster, but that year they were all incredibly large. Between sporadic gasps of air, I was underwater for the majority of the rapid before eventually resurfacing.

The entire area below the rapid was flooded and churning right up to the next rapid on the river, known as Dog's Leg. Without my kayak, I was much less able to maneuver in the water, and I was heading straight for the worst part of Dog's Leg. Luckily, there was another kayaker who was resting in some of the calmer water to the side of the main river, and he paddled out to where I was so I could grab onto the back of his kayak. He pulled me away from the worst part of Dog's Leg so that I could float down through the center.

Thousands of kayakers and white-water rafters go down the Ottawa River each year, so I know the mortality risk was actually very low, but it was a frightening experience all around. And it must have been particularly traumatic on a psychological level because of how it affected me in the subsequent weeks and months. Whenever I would think about kayaking, I would immediately get a feeling of anxiety and emotional dread. My mind had flagged kayaking as a serious threat, so the mere thought of it would trigger the fight-or-flight response within me.

I allowed that mental association to persist for longer than I should have, and I avoided kayaking for a time. But, as with my experience with social phobia, I could see how avoidance was just solidifying my newfound phobia. The avoidance itself was contributing to my mental justification that kayaking was a real threat. I knew I had to do something about it. I went back to the Ottawa River and purposely went down through the Coliseum Rapid again to overwrite the fear connection that had been created in my mind.

After I voluntarily faced the situation again and breathed through it with a calmer mindset, the emotional connection was altered. I now do not get the same fear-based emotions surfacing when I think about kayaking. Unfortunately, I think I had left it too long for my mental rewiring to be fully effective. I have kayaked a number of times since then, but there seems to be a small amount of lingering anxiety from that experience.

Phobias

Humans and animals have a natural fight-or-flight response system that allows us to react quickly to environmental threats that may cause us pain or death. This system plays a critical role in keeping us alive, since real threats exist in the world around us. In the case of most phobias, however, our fight-or-flight response system is either activated by an irrational fear or becomes overly intensified. The magnitude of our emotional reactions does not match the real magnitude of the threat in these instances. In other words, the phobic response is unwarranted and illogical, often interfering with daily life and normal physiological functioning.

We are born with only two innate phobias—the fear of falling and the fear of loud sounds—but most of us soon develop additional phobias from observing others and from learned experiences. There has been some interesting research into whether the fear of spiders and snakes is also innate, since this fear was important for primate survival and is so common in adults. However, images of spiders and snakes shown to babies don't seem to elicit a fear response, only dilated pupils and a heightened interest.

It is often difficult to pinpoint the particular origin of phobias; even significant introspection and professional help discerning the roots is generally inconclusive. This is because phobias are often linked to childhood experiences that we may not even remember, or only partially remember. The most easily identified origins of phobias are from traumas experienced either during childhood or at other points in our lives. Our minds make interesting connections and mental associations, though, so the incident may be pointedly different than what currently triggers the fear response. Phobias can be either minor inconveniences or they can be extremely debilitating, depending on the specific phobia and severity. Common phobias include insects, dogs, flying, enclosed spaces, driving, heights, thunder, needles, the sight of blood, public speaking, and clowns, although people can develop phobias to literally anything, including imaginary things.

Individuals who are high in neuroticism and low in extraversion are particularly susceptible to social phobias and agoraphobia.

For individuals who have developed phobias to one or more things, exposure to those things, or even the thought of exposure, often produces anxiety, intense fear, and panic sensations. The fear can be debilitating, as it is often accompanied by behavioral and functional difficulties, sweating, tight chest, rapid heart rate, nausea, dizziness, and a whole slew of other physical and psychological changes. I know these sensations and limitations well, having lived with GAD for a good portion of my life.

There is a fair bit of research suggesting that our biology and genetics play a significant role in our predisposition to phobias. Many members of my extended family have suffered from anxiety—some still do. I remember my grandfather often saying how much he loathed having to speak in public, and others in the family have had similar issues, including me, as you know. But because we are very good at picking up on subtle body language, especially when we are children, fears can be adopted without ever having been discussed, simply from watching facial expressions and mannerisms. This is one reason hereditary conclusions are so difficult to make. It is almost impossible to isolate certain variables.

I haven't been as affected by phobias as some people, but I've been more affected than most, and I've been able to overcome many phobias—including those of, to varying degrees, heights, spiders, being trapped, needles, failure, authority figures, and a few other more short-lived ones. I learned a lot working through each of these, and I want to stress the importance of not allowing phobias to get a foothold in our lives. We need to be aware of the onset of phobias, guard against it, and work hard to intervene early. When we notice the early indicators, we have the opportunity to address them proactively. After phobias have taken root and integrated into our psyche, it is more difficult to overcome them, and there may be aspects that linger with us that we never truly transcend.

Exposure Therapy

What I had put myself through, by going kayaking after my phobia had developed, was a form of exposure therapy—a *systematic desensitization* therapy originally developed by South African psychiatrist Joseph Wolpe in 1958. Since then, there have been many variations developed in its application, but the basic premise behind it has generally been accepted as the most effective treatment for overcoming phobias.

With exposure therapy, the foundational idea is that the sufferer is gradually and voluntarily exposed to the stimulus that causes the irrational fear. Moving too quickly can be traumatic and even counterproductive depending on the severity of the phobia, especially if the sufferer hasn't really embraced the technique. It could be argued that for my kayaking phobia, a more gradual method of exposure therapy would be to first picture myself calmly going back down through the same rapid, then to look at a photograph of myself going through the rapid, then to do some kayaking in calm water before exposing myself to the situation I was fearful of. The speed and severity of exposure need to be based on the comfort level of the sufferer; there isn't really a catch-all solution.

A major advantage of exposure therapy is that it is effective even when the origins of the phobia are unknown. It isn't necessary to dig into a person's past experiences and upbringing, for example—although that isn't to say that understanding past events has no merit. In a clinical environment, a trained psychologist or psychotherapist guides the patient through the exposure therapy process, and many people find such practitioner relationships to be very valuable.

I am a big advocate of exposure therapy, as you can probably tell from my personal experiences. I used this approach in working through my anxiety disorder and social phobia, also referred to as social anxiety disorder (SAD), so I can vouch for it. Depending on the challenges you may be experiencing, forms of exposure therapy are also effective for treating post-traumatic stress disorder (PTSD) and obsessive-compulsive disorder (OCD).

One important thing to remember is that the exposure has to be done consciously and voluntarily. Forcing someone to face their fear often just intensifies it. An example of this would be throwing rubber snakes at someone who has a snake phobia. It may be entertaining for the person throwing the snakes, but it doesn't help the person who has the phobia in the least. If the person were to voluntarily handle a rubber snake, though, that could be a first step in exposure therapy.

What is important in the process is that there is a change in the phobic individual's response to the stimuli, even if the change is subtle. This helps to rewrite the experience as a less threatening one in the mind of the phobic. Combining exposure therapy with one or more relaxation techniques, a few of which we will cover later in this chapter, can speed up the process and augment the effectiveness.

Cognitive Distortions

When we have a phobia, our natural tendency is to minimize our perceived ability to cope with the stimuli and maximize our perceived failures. These distorted thought patterns are errors in our thoughts, beliefs, and attitudes, and are known as *cognitive distortions*. The story that I opened this book with, about my envisioning catastrophic outcomes at the conference I was attending, is a real-life example of how cognitive distortions can become ingrained in our automatic thought patterns.

Correcting cognitive distortions is a key component of cognitive behavioral therapy (CBT), a psychological treatment approach pioneered by psychiatrists Aaron Beck and David Burns. CBT is an approach many psychotherapists and counselors use with patients to treat a wide range of psychological disorders. I won't go into CBT in a lot of detail—there are whole books available on it—but I do want to mention a few of the most common cognitive distortions. This knowledge can be tremendously beneficial in recognizing our own roadblocks when it comes to overcoming phobias, so that we can take action in manipulating them.

COGNITIVE FILTERING occurs when we filter out the positive aspects of a situation and focus only on the negative aspects. This has an evolutionary basis, since avoiding negative situations was more important in keeping our ancestors alive than seeking out positive ones. Cognitive filtering is a cognitive distortion that I fall victim to particularly often. An example from my kayak incident would be to recall only the negative feelings, or a particular negative feeling, associated with kayaking, while ignoring the positive elements of excitement and adventure that brought me to enjoy the sport in the first place.

OVERGENERALIZATION is when we make overarching conclusions about something based on an isolated incident or isolated evidence. In my kayaking example, overgeneralization would be if I concluded that I am a failure of an athlete and should quit adventure sports altogether because of my single defeat.

CATASTROPHIZING OR MAGNIFYING is when we expect that the outcome will be disastrous, always imagining the worst possible conclusion. This cognitive distortion prevents people from taking part in all kinds of activities, even everyday ones like driving or flying. In my kayaking example, if I were catastrophizing, I might imagine drowning and death every time I envisioned myself kayaking.

POLARIZED THINKING is when we end up thinking in all-or-nothing terms, without considering any intermediate outcomes. This is the Star Wars Sith mentality of dealing in absolutes, exemplified in Anakin Skywalker's response during his confrontation with Obi-Wan Kenobi: "If you're not with me, then you're my enemy!" In my kayaking example, this might involve me envisioning myself as a failure if I felt any sort of anxiety about the experience. Or I might think I need a perfect execution of the rapid in order for it to be considered a success.

There are various other cognitive distortions to be aware of; these are just a few of the most common ones—and ones that I have often succumbed to. If you recognize one or more of these cognitive distortions, the key is to notice them, refute them, and—ideally—replace them with more realistic and positive representations. This process is known as cognitive restructuring and can be done individually or with the help of a therapist.

Emotional Influence

The first step to having any kind of influence over our emotional responses is to realize that there is a space between the situations we find ourselves in, or more accurately the stimuli sensed in these situations, and our emotional response. For most people this space is not very large, and for some it seems to not exist at all. The space I'm referring to is our window of opportunity to interject and influence our emotional responses.

An example of this space might be the few seconds between when someone steals your parking spot and the anger that wells up inside of you, or even explodes verbally from you. People who have no influence over their emotional responses will predictably feel and react the same way each time they experience this or a similar situation. But those who have expanded and managed this space can affect emotional responses in many different ways. The most obvious application of this influence is to have some control on regulating the emotions we experience ourselves, but once we understand more about emotions, we are also able to have more influence on the emotional responses of others.

Psychologist James Gross developed a framework that I really like for better understanding and visualizing the different ways that we can regulate emotions. It is called the process model of emotion regulation, and it illustrates the space that I'm referring to as well as the points of potential influence that exist between the emotional stimuli and our emotional responses. In Dr. Gross's model, there are five regulating processes by which we can influence emotional responses: situation selection, situation modification, attention deployment, cognitive change, and response modulation.

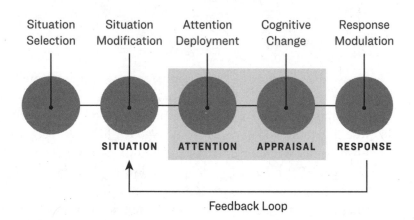

REGULATING EMOTIONS
James Gross's Process Model of Emotion Regulation

Adapted from J.J. Gross

Let's say that your boss at work is angry at you and leaves a note on your desk to come into their office immediately. How might the regulating process work?

The first option is to regulate emotion through *situation selection*, which in this case is fairly self-explanatory. If you choose to approach your boss, you are going to experience the emotions associated with the encounter. You could also avoid the situation, which gives you a totally different emotional response. There are practical considerations here—avoiding the situation may just defer the emotional response and could perhaps even intensify it at a later time.

The second option is to regulate your emotion through *situation modification*. This may include calling your boss on the phone, for example, or distancing yourself in another way. Perhaps you could wait until the situation can be dealt with in a team meeting or in another less intimidating environment. You may also be able to smooth the situation by altering the subject, bringing in humor, or starting the conversation on a high note where you have some common ground.

The third option is to regulate your emotion through *attention deployment*. On the negative side of attention deployment, you can allow your full attention to be hijacked by the situation, likely resulting in excessive rumination and worry. On the flip side, instead of allowing your attention to be consumed by the situation, you could find distractions or apply thought suppression to direct your attention, using attention deployment to influence your emotional response in a positive manner. This may involve thinking about something else, distracting yourself with other work, or talking to a colleague.

The fourth option is to regulate your emotion through *cognitive change*. In my view, this is the most important area of change for deep emotional influence. However, it takes years for our automatic thought patterns to develop, so it isn't easy to change them, and won't likely happen overnight. A cognitive change might be reappraising the situation to see it through a different lens—for example, you might see the situation as your boss wanting to help you with constructive criticism because you are a valuable team member. Or perhaps you see the anger as a coping mechanism for your boss to cover up their own inadequacies, and you empathize with them. There are an infinite number of different reappraisals that could be applied to how you are viewing the situation. In my own mental health journey, I had to make a lot of deep cognitive changes, and I think this is the most important and long-lasting way to influence and regulate our emotions.

The last option is to regulate your emotion through *response modulation*. If you've gotten to this step, you've already experienced the emotion, but there are ways to modulate the outcome. If you are having persistent negative emotions about encounters with your boss over the long term, modulation may involve fixing your sleep patterns or getting more exercise. Another fairly simple response modulation technique is to change your body language. Most of us understand that our thoughts affect our emotions, which affect our body language. When we are thinking sad or depressing thoughts, we might show it by looking down and slouching our shoulders, for example. What many of us don't understand is that the relationship also has a reverse effect. If we convince ourselves to stand up straight, hold our shoulders back, and put a smile on our face, there is a biofeedback loop to our brain that back-drives the whole system by changing our emotions and ultimately affecting our thought patterns as well. Dr. Erik Peper has done some interesting research on this biofeedback to our brains based on posture. One of his findings was that our posture also affects our memory recall in addition to our overall mood.

It is important to remember that our emotional response progression is an iterative cycle: each emotional response becomes part of our new situation, so it gets fed back into the cycle as a stimulus for subsequent emotions. This may help you understand how the positive feedback loops that I was outlining earlier are formed and how our emotions and thought patterns can easily become self-fulfilling prophecies.

I want to outline some of the various techniques that I have personally used throughout my life for self-regulation of emotions and thought patterns. Feel free to learn from them, modify them, and apply them in whatever ways are beneficial for you, or disregard them if you don't find them helpful. I didn't invent all of these techniques, but I've adapted and revised many of them to make methods that worked for me. Their foundations are derived from techniques that are broadly recommended and used by practitioners.

For all the techniques that I studied and read about, I would often try them out for an adequate amount of time to be able to judge for myself whether I thought they were helpful or not. I felt silly at times practicing these techniques, but I tried to approach them with an open mind. If you're going through your own mental health–related challenges or just want to be able to better regulate your emotions, I would recommend you do the same. Find out what works for you by continuing to experiment and learn by paying attention to, and ideally documenting, your own experience and feedback. The goal is to add strategies that work for you to your future toolkit.

I'm afraid I can't pinpoint for sure which techniques were the most beneficial, although I particularly like the cognitive defusion technique that I shared in the Summit of Self-Knowledge. A combination of these techniques seemed to work well for me: I didn't see amazing results immediately from any one; they were all part of my journey of making gradual changes and small improvements in many areas of my life. Recall what I mentioned at the beginning of this book: There is no quick fix. If you still think you're going to stumble upon a radical technique that turns your life around, you'll most likely be disappointed over and over again. The answer is a holistic one found through small, purposeful changes.

Mindfulness

In all of this, a key is to pay attention and be aware of what's going on with you. The most focused version of this is what is called *mindfulness*. Some people are skeptical of this method. I'm not anymore.

Let me tell you about a short experience that I had that really cemented my belief in the utility and benefits of mindfulness practices. It was an experience I had on a flight a number of years ago. Meditation was pretty new to me at that time, although I had been reading a lot about it; I was still actively working through challenges with anxiety and depression, so I was willing to try anything that may be helpful, and I was doing my best to give mindfulness practices a fair test. At the same time, I was, in some ways, in constant conflict with myself: part of my mind was always pulling me away from practicing mindfulness techniques to do something more productive, so I would try to get through the exercises as quickly as possible. This was, of course, counterproductive.

The particular experience I remember, I was on a long-haul flight, late at night, and I had been reading for a few hours. I was quite relaxed and didn't have anything else on my mind except the contents of the book. I decided to stop reading for a few minutes and just allow my mind to be empty and still. I stared up at a blank spot on the aircraft ceiling and just let everything go. I had practiced meditation techniques before and reached relatively deep states of relaxation, but this particular time I entered into a new level of complete stillness, deeper than I had ever experienced before. It is difficult to put into words what happened, but it was a distinct level of inner peace. Not only did I not consciously have any worries, but somehow even my deeper apprehensions dissolved. It was a state of blissful nothingness, and I felt fantastic in those moments.

Unfortunately, that incredible state didn't last too long; once I really started to notice how good I felt, my mind started wondering how I had gotten there. I tried to ignore these more evaluative thoughts, but it was too late—the experience had passed, and I was back to conscious evaluation. And I've never since been able to get all the way back to that state of profound inner peace. Perhaps it was just the right combination of what I was reading combined with my circumstances and surroundings at the time. But I have read a bit about the quest for enlightenment, and I think I got a glimpse of what *enlightenment* is referring to.

Mindfulness is a psychological practice that has roots in Buddhist traditions, although nowadays there are many secular mindfulness practices as well. Even in the absence of religion, however, there is a spiritual element in the way that mindfulness allows us to connect with our deeper selves. Mindfulness is all about conscious awareness of the present moment, rather than dwelling in the past or rehearsing future events. There is also an acceptance aspect of mindfulness, which is why it is often considered a branch of positive psychology. It is a nonjudgmental observation of one's thoughts, feelings, sensations, and environment—a moment-to-moment awareness of our mental and physical presence.

The Western world can largely thank Jon Kabat-Zinn for bringing mindfulness to prominence, or at least popularizing it in a wide range of applications, for its therapeutic and stress reduction benefits. He developed the Mindfulness-Based Stress Reduction (MBSR) program at the University of Massachusetts Medical School, variations of which are now used in hospitals, schools, prisons, clinics, and many other sectors.

The tangible physical, emotional, spiritual, and psychological benefits of practicing mindfulness are abundant, which is why it has become so popular. Some of the benefits that have been discovered from empirical studies of mindfulness include reduction in stress and anxiety, reduced mental rumination, improved focus, increased satisfaction in relationships, improved immune function, better sleep quality, increased self-awareness and social awareness, and improvements to working memory. If you are looking for a relatively straightforward place to start in working towards any of these improvements in your own life, mindfulness is probably one of the best places to start.

Getting the most out of mindfulness does take time and practice, however. It can be hard to focus on the present moment. If you think that you already do, you are most likely incorrect. Psychologists Matthew Killingsworth and Daniel Gilbert published a study of 2,250 participants in 2010 and found that people's minds wandered quite frequently—46.9 percent of the time, the subjects studied were not paying attention to what was right in front of them. We spend almost half of our waking lives envisioning past or future scenarios rather than being in the present.

The basics of mindfulness are straightforward. Any time you wish to be more mindful, it is a matter of bringing your attention to the present moment. This may sound quite simple, and on one level it is, but our minds easily wander, and if you are not used to practicing mindfulness, you will most likely find your mind wandering to past or future scenarios or questioning and evaluating what you are doing within a few seconds of beginning, and before you know it you are no longer present.

But the goal of mindfulness is not to direct your mind. It is just to pay attention to the present without judgment. When judgments arise, simply let them roll by without engaging them. You'll need a degree of kindness so that you don't get angry or annoyed by how frequently your mind tries to wander. Mindfulness involves returning, again and again, to present-moment observation.

Begin by noticing subtle body sensations, without evaluating or judging. These might include a tingling feeling, an itch, or a warm or cold area of your body. Take in your surroundings through each of your senses. What do you smell? What do you hear? If your eyes are open, what do you see? If you are touching or leaning against something, how does it feel? Do you have any taste in your mouth? Just observe these sensory aspects.

Next, what emotions are you currently feeling? Don't try to figure out *why* you are feeling these emotions, just allow them to be present. Take note of them and allow them to come or go as they please.

Do you have any current urges or cravings? Notice them without acting on them. Gently redirect your attention back to the present, over and over again, every time your mind wanders. Observe the integration and flow of all these different aspects of your body and mind. Continue to pay attention and be present.

If you can do this for a few minutes, you will notice right away the calming and focusing benefits of mindfulness. This is the essence that all mindfulness techniques are built upon, although there are many variations and different ways of getting there.

Mindful Breathing

Mindful breathing can be considered one of the foundational mindfulness techniques, and if you are new to practicing self-regulation, this is an excellent first step. It may be basic, but it's effective. Even advanced meditation classes incorporate mindful breathing into their routine. I have used it many times, and continue to do so, for reducing stress as well as calming and focusing my body and mind.

Begin by putting your body in a restful position, ideally either sitting comfortably or lying down. You can either close your eyes or rest them in a neutral position, gazing at something that won't be distracting.

Bring your attention to your breath—inhaling and exhaling—along with the associated sensations. Perhaps you can feel the rise and fall of your chest, the warm or tickling sensation within your nostrils or throat, and how the air feels as it passes through your nostrils or over your lips.

Take long slow breaths in and out, especially on exhaling. A good rule to follow is the 4-7-8 breathing technique: breathe in for four seconds, hold the breath for seven seconds, and then breathe out for eight seconds. If you need some assistance with the cadence, there are many apps that can help guide you through your practice.

Give this a try, and you will be surprised at how such a simple and straightforward technique can calm and focus your body and mind.

Deliberate Contemplation

Deliberate contemplation isn't technically a mindfulness technique, as it involves directing and channeling thoughts towards a specific purpose rather than observing. As I touched on when exploring cognitive defusion, this is an active process that takes energy and can be mentally exhausting, so it should be practiced only in deliberate time periods. It is for developing mental discipline more than learning how to relax. If you find your mind frequently flipping back and forth between different challenges and your inability to focus is frustrating you, this technique helps develop the capacity to channel your thinking.

With deliberate contemplation, choose an object or a theme and try to let your mind focus and think only about that particular object or theme. The simpler the object, often the more difficult it is to continue the contemplation without allowing your mind to wander. For example, I might choose to contemplate a glass of water, a mosquito, a potato chip, or any other random object. The object itself isn't particularly important; it is the mental discipline that you are trying to develop.

When I have used this technique, I set a timer for five or ten minutes and only allow myself to contemplate the object I've chosen during that time period. I sometimes first think of the color, texture, and other characteristics of the object. Then I think about possible uses for the object. Then I think of where one would buy or find the object, or where it was made. The whole point is to just continue thinking about the same thing.

It probably sounds fairly easy, but because our minds are easily distracted and tend to wander, we start to get bored and soon other thoughts enter our mind. Where deliberate contemplation is like mindfulness techniques is that you then bring your attention back to what you are contemplating, over and over again. Your wandering mind may be a bit frustrating, since it seems like this should be a simple task, but you will notice improvement with practice.

Deliberate contemplation has a lot of related practical uses and benefits when it comes to focusing on real-life challenges and solutions without getting distracted. We waste a lot of time and energy when our minds are flipping back and forth randomly between various challenges.

Picture Frame Technique

There are two ways you can apply the picture frame technique, and I've found both to be beneficial. The first way alters your emotional reaction to past events, where the memory of such events currently prompts negative and unwanted emotions. The second way is to prepare for and preprogram your emotional reaction to future events that you are currently anxious about or where you have been envisioning negative outcomes.

Regardless of whether the event is future or past, what you do is envision the situation in your mind's eye—but instead of viewing it close-up or through your own eyes, consciously stop and zoom out in your mind, so that you are watching it from an elevated or distanced view. If you still feel the anxiety, imagine that you are watching the scenario unfold through a picture frame.

Once you can view the scenario through the picture frame without the negative emotions, slowly zoom back in, continuing to play the scenario over and over again in your mind and observing your emotions. You may need to zoom out again and go through a few iterations, but eventually you work on moving slowly closer until you are envisioning the scenario unfold from the vantage point of your own eyes, but without the unwanted emotional reactions.

This technique seems to disassociate your mental imagery from your negative emotions, which not only helps whenever you are remembering or daydreaming about past events, but also helps reduce negative associative connections for related future scenarios. In my experience, it requires commitment to frequent repetition and careful diligence in avoiding cognitive distortions and negative self-talk. Half-hearted efforts will yield lukewarm results. But it can have far-reaching life benefits: the emotional and mental shifts can extend to other encounters and experiences beyond the particular experience focused on during the technique.

You will find it relatively easy to identify which past events you should primarily focus on. Simply recall past situations in your mind or envision future situations, picturing each as an image or a mental movie. When you feel anxiety, panic, anger, fear, discomfort, or another negative response, you know that particular situation is one worth focusing on.

Rewriting the Ending

A variation to the picture frame technique involves rewriting the endings associated with troublesome past scenarios. I have applied this technique successfully from the picture frame perspective, from a third-person perspective, and from a first-person perspective, often working through all three perspectives sequentially.

The goal of this technique is to dissolve the associative connections between the negative emotions and past events. Imagine a scenario as you would with the picture frame technique, but use your imagination to picture yourself ending the scenario how you would have liked it to end. Although this is make-believe, it alters the feelings that you have associated with the scenario, and this is where the benefit is. Whenever I practice this technique, it seems to leave me better equipped for improved emotional reactions when I am faced with similar future scenarios. At the very least, my mind is able to see that there are other, positive conclusions that can take place, so I am less apprehensive about similar situations in the future.

I have used an adaptation of this rewriting technique for future scenarios as well. It may seem like there is nothing to rewrite in the case of future events, but we have often pre-written a negative narrative through unrestrained forethought. For example, in my past when I found out that I had to make a public appearance, my mind would immediately go into disaster-thinking mode—as in the scenario I started this book with. In these instances, when I would have a chance to spend some time in relaxed thinking, I would decide how I wanted the future scenario to end, and then I would run that new ending through my mind over and over again to attempt to rewrite the negative version.

Like the other techniques I'm sharing, the results aren't particularly drastic or immediate, but with practice and persistence you can benefit as I did.

Self-Love and Encouragement Technique

This is another visualization technique for altering the automatic onset of negative emotions associated with past memories. Like the picture frame and rewriting techniques, you first start by picturing yourself going through a past scenario, the memory of which still induces negative emotion. This time though, picture your current self approaching the past version of yourself that is in your mental movie.

I often used this technique for childhood and adolescent situations that still bothered me. I would envision my adult self approaching the anxious, trembling boy that was my younger self, so there would be two versions of me in the mental movie. I would then picture my current self consoling and encouraging the past version of myself. I would talk to the past version of myself, explaining to him that everything was OK and there was no need to be anxious or afraid. I would often even give the past version of myself a hug in my mental movie and do everything I could to reassure him.

If you have seen some of the recent Star Trek movies, this technique is a bit like the past and present versions of Spock conversing with each other. It is a strange concept, and you may feel silly applying it, but if you can watch it at the theater, then you can certainly practice it in your own mind. It is an odd way of altering emotional memories, but it worked in my life. You have nothing to lose in trying it, and I think you will be surprised at its effectiveness.

It is relatively easy to determine whether you have been successful with any of the three techniques I have just shared. All you have to do is run the scenarios through your mind at any time, and if your emotional response has been altered or diminished, you have made progress. I saw that they were working for me, and that encouraged me to keep doing them and trying different variations.

Identifying the Positives

The technique of identifying the positives can be applied periodically or during short time periods you set aside, but it is most effective when it becomes your habitual way of observing and thinking about things throughout your day-to-day interactions. Choose a time each day to stop what you are doing and take ten minutes to identify the positive things that are happening in your work, your family, your relationships, your community, and more broadly in life. Don't lose hope; you'll be able to find positive elements no matter how bad things may seem. Keep it up so you can expand the technique to develop it into a regular habit.

In addition to the mood-regulating reasons for identifying the positives, there are highly practical reasons as well. Of the millions of signals we receive though our five senses— touching, seeing, hearing, smelling, and tasting—we are only able to consciously process a small fraction. We just don't have the cognitive capabilities, so we are not consciously aware of the vast majority of sensory signals we receive. If we think of just our vision, for example, in the fovea centralis of our eyes, we have an array of densely packed cones that give us sharp vision for determining details. We direct our eyes towards things we are interested in, and we process the light that filters in. But this foveal vision accounts for only about 1.5 to 2 degrees of our visual field. The vast majority of our vision is peripheral, where we have a sparser array of cone cells and less representation in our visual cortex. We generally ignore almost everything in our peripheral vision unless we catch a glimpse of fast movement, the outline of a potential threat, or something particularly relevant to us, in which case we quickly move our eyes to align our foveal vision.

Focusing on the positive elements influences *what* you notice and process. When you're constantly focused on the negative elements, you tend to notice more negative aspects around you. If you're working on a project, for example, and are prone to perpetual negative thinking, you notice and concentrate on all the factors that will get in your way or prevent you from bringing the project to fruition. The many small, almost imperceptible roadblocks that might otherwise remain unprocessed become amplified. You are *problem focused* in this case and, sure enough, you notice more and more roadblocks.

If, on the other hand, you are constantly focused on identifying the positive aspects, you begin to notice the positive elements and successes all around you, and you can take advantage of all the many small positive aspects that help you bring your end goals to fruition. You are *solution focused* in this case and, sure enough, you notice more and more solutions.

This is just how our brains are wired. If you are focused on spiders, for example, your senses become hyperaware of any sensation that may resemble a spider. Things that would generally go unnoticed, such as the slight tickle-feeling of something brushing against your back or a black dot in the corner of the room, all of a sudden come front and center as soon as you sense them.

Especially if you are the type of person who is frequently focused on the negative, it is worth making a commitment to gradually shift your tendencies towards positivity. Along with its positive effect on your own experience of life, it will positively affect your social relationships. I've worked with what I refer to as "dark cloud people," who seem to have an aura of negativity that rains down on everyone and everything around them. Positive people are so much better to have around us.

Body Scan Meditation

Body scan meditation is a relaxation and refocusing technique that I still use fairly frequently, most commonly when I am trying to fall asleep but my mind is racing. It helps to release physical and psychological tension by progressively relaxing each area of your body. I generally run through the meditation in my head, but there are many guided versions that you can download in audio format or view online as well, some of which I have used in the past.

Start in a comfortable position, ideally lying down, and slowly bring your attention to your feet. Notice any tension in your feet and mentally visualize the tension melting away. You can focus on one side of your body at a time or both together. It is helpful to combine this mental visualization with repetition of phrases, aloud or in your mind. Repeat to yourself, "My feet feel loose, heavy, and relaxed," and visualize your feet sinking down into the surface beneath them.

Once your feet are relaxed, continue moving up your body, scanning and relaxing one area at a time. Repeat the same visualization and self-talk with your calf muscles, your knees, your thighs, and each area of your body in sequence until you get to the top of your head. If you have given yourself adequate time and attention, at the end of this meditation your entire body will feel relaxed and free of tension.

If you have never tried body scan meditation, give it a try tonight as you are trying to relax in bed. You may be pleasantly surprised—or you may not notice because you have already fallen asleep.

Progressive Muscle Relaxation

The technique of progressive muscle relaxation is primarily for releasing muscle tension, but I find it has psychological relaxation benefits as well. It is similar to body scan meditation; the goal is to focus on one muscle group at a time, and I generally start with my feet.

Again, start in a comfortable position, ideally lying down, and first tense the muscles in your feet, holding them in tension for around five seconds. Then release the tension and wait ten seconds in a state of relaxation before moving on to your calf muscles. Tense each muscle group, one at a time, as you move all the way from your feet up to your head.

Notice the difference between the tensed and relaxed states of your muscles. This is an important part of the meditation. When you release each muscle group, visualize and feel the muscles relaxing. This can be combined with the same repetition of inaudible or audible phrases that I mentioned in the body scan meditation technique. There are lots of guided variations of this technique online as well if you want to experiment with a few different ways of completing the meditation.

I have found this technique especially beneficial when I have particularly tense, aching, or throbbing muscles to begin with, which is sometimes the case when I have overworked them—or after I have been sedentary for long periods of time.

Mental Vacations

The last technique I want to recommend is taking a vacation. I don't mean going to Hawaii and swimming with the manta rays, though that's also worth doing; I mean taking a mental vacation. Get your mind off your current reality by allowing your thoughts and imagination to take you psychologically away to a different place. Ideally, this should be a place free of stress where you can relax and settle your mind. There are many different ways to take a mental vacation: read a book, get lost in a movie, listen to music, walk through nature... Even forms of daydreaming are mental vacations, as long as you don't ruminate on something negative or become engrossed in problem solving. The challenge usually isn't finding an avenue for a mental vacation; the challenge instead is carving out the time and committing to actually doing it periodically.

But you also need to be aware that there is a limit to how often you should indulge in this technique. I've met people who seem to be on a perpetual mental vacation, lost in la-la land and oblivious to reality, which isn't good either. There are healthy ways to embrace the concept of mental vacations and there are unhealthy ways—there is a balance like there is for many of the other concepts we've been exploring.

Expedition Debrief

We have explored a number of practical self-regulation exercises in this chapter that you can practice in your own life, and I hope that you experience the same gains that I have. You will want to check in and debrief yourself along the way about what is working, what is not working, and what you should continue to work on, because your own feedback can help to refine and focus your efforts.

What are the phobias that you need to address in your life? Are you willing to go through the steps involved in working through these phobias in order to be free of them? The process can be scary, but the life benefits are well worth the commitment. Remember the principles and importance of exposure therapy and correcting cognitive distortions as you deliberately and incrementally rewire your automatic thought patterns.

Do you find you are frequently ruminating over past events or are stuck in a cycle of future worrying? There can be benefit in past and future envisioning, but life happens in the present, so don't miss it. Mindfulness techniques should be your focus if you are stuck in your own mental wanderings and need to center yourself more in the here and now.

Lastly, give the self-regulation techniques that I detailed a genuine chance. If you can, commit to practicing one of them for a number of weeks without failing before you make up your mind on its effectiveness. I found that quality repetition of singular techniques was more effective in my life than the quantity of techniques I would try to fit. The more you practice self-regulation, the better you will be at the techniques and the quicker you will be able to regulate your own emotions.

Eventually, you will start to see which techniques bring you the most benefit so that no matter which mountain you are facing, you will have the right tools at your disposal to confidently and level-headedly make your ascent. There are enough storms that are beyond your control; you don't need inner storms as well to further complicate circumstances. Once you become good at quieting your inner turmoil, you will find you are in a much better place to deal with the outer turmoil.

THE SUMMIT OF SELF-RESPECT

The Rental Skis

Rental skis taught me an important lesson in self-respect.

A few years ago, I found myself speaking at an event in Boise, Idaho, at the end of January, right in the heart of ski season. I had an extra day, so I took a rental car up to Sun Valley Resort, just a few hours east of Boise.

Once I arrived at my hotel in the little village of Ketchum, I called up one of the local shops to inquire about renting skis for the following day. The owner was a young man who was quite accommodating; he hadn't closed his shop just yet for the night and said if I wanted to come by that evening, he would rent me a pair. He even said I could leave them at my hotel room after my day of skiing and he would pick them up from the hotel, which I thought sounded pretty convenient and accommodating.

I drove over to his ski shop and he set up a pair of beautiful powder skis that looked to be brand new, without a scratch on them. The owner and I had similar interests, and we ended up chatting for a while about why I was in the area and about what I do for a living. He gave me an excellent price on the ski rental, and I had cash with me, so I paid him up front. I threw the skis over my shoulder and started heading for the door, but I realized I hadn't given him a damage deposit or any information about me. I turned and asked if he wanted a credit card imprint or anything like that. He replied with a smile, "No, I trust you."

The next day was a fantastic day of carving through fresh, fluffy powder. I had a fabulous time. But when I finished my last run for the day and took off my skis, I noticed something protruding from the bottom of one of them. I took a look and, to my surprise and dismay, there was a long, deep gouge along the bottom of the ski and a large chunk of the base plastic was missing, exposing the core.

My heart sank as I stared at the damage I had done to that beautiful pair of skis. I started to imagine how I would feel if someone had damaged my skis to that degree and the repercussions I would be facing. How could I return the skis in that condition? Would I have to purchase them at full price—and would it even be worth shipping the skis home, or would I simply have to fork out the money and leave them? I drove back to my hotel feeling awful about the whole situation.

Part of me wanted to avoid any kind of additional contact with the ski shop owner and just get on the plane the next day, leaving him to deal with the situation. After all, he hadn't taken an imprint of my credit card. He had no recourse. He had even explicitly said I could leave the skis in the hotel and he would pick them up. Wasn't this the risk he took in renting skis anyways? I was engaged in a moral tug-of-war. As much as I wanted to avoid the costs, embarrassment, and consequences, I also didn't feel right about sneaking away like that. I drove around the village for a while, pondering what I could do. I even stopped by a local thrift store and purchased an old kitchen knife that I thought I might be able to use to remove the jagged ripples of plastic and repair some of the damage. It didn't really work, though—in many ways it just made it look worse.

In the end my moral conscience won, and I decided to head back to the ski shop and return the skis directly. As much as I dreaded having to do so, I would simply have to pay for the damage I had caused—or buy the skis outright.

I arrived at the shop and was greeted by the friendly shop owner, who asked me how my ski day had been. I told him it was superb, and he immediately grabbed the skis, which I had leaned against the counter, and put them back on the ski rack.

Was it really that easy? I had delivered them—wasn't it his responsibility to inspect them? He probably wouldn't even remember who he had rented them to now that they were with the rest of the skis on the rack. A second round of tug-of-war took place inside my head within a few short moments. My heart was pounding in my chest from the moral dilemma; I continued to talk with the shop owner cordially, but most of my attention was on my internal dialogue. He thanked me for renting from him and said to come on back if I was ever in the area again.

I started to leave but I just couldn't do it. I had to turn back and face the issue head-on. I walked back and began to confess in a sheepish voice the damage I had caused. I pulled the skis back off of the rack and showed him the bottom of the ski, which looked even worse in the lights of his shop.

"What did you do?" he exclaimed, but surprisingly still with a smile on his face. He came over and had a good look at the damage. He didn't seem particularly angry, though, and invited me to come through to the back of his shop where he had his equipment. Believe it or not, he actually thanked me sincerely as we were walking for letting him know about the damage so he didn't accidentally rent a damaged ski to the next customer. He placed the ski in a clamp and plugged in what looked like a large glue gun. As we continued chatting, he took out a razor blade and started cutting away the plastic all around the damaged area, removing any jagged sections. He then used the glorified glue gun, which presumably was some sort of liquid-plastic applicator, to fill in the section he had just opened up, smoothing over the plastic as he worked. When he was done, he put the ski on the bench, leaving the newly applied plastic facing upwards to dry.

I apologized again and asked him how much I owed him for the damage. To my surprise, he said I didn't owe him a thing and thanked me again for my honesty. He did mention that he would like to read more about my family's Everest expedition sometime, as we had chatted earlier about it. I had a few copies in my rental car, so I ran out and got one—I was happy to give him a signed copy. It didn't repay the damage, but I thought it was the least I could do after the whole ordeal. We shook hands and parted ways cheerfully and on good terms.

As I was driving away from the ski shop, I felt a sense of contentment and even self-pride. In spite of being tempted to do what would have been the easy and expedient thing, I had taken the more difficult and arguably more respectable route, and I was at peace with myself.

I don't share this story about my ski rental experience to make myself look virtuous or to pass moral judgments, because the truth is I can't say I have always taken the high ground. But every time I have taken the easy road, it has eroded my self-respect and led to feelings of regret and emptiness inside. This is why it is so important for us to do what we feel to be morally right. The inner consequences associated with not doing so far outweigh any external consequences that we may be trying to avoid.

Our relationship with ourselves is the most important relationship we have, and we shouldn't take it for granted. We also shouldn't be so naive as to think that this self-relationship cannot be damaged. I've met many people who have developed a deep self-loathing and have lost complete respect for themselves through many years of failed convictions and moral blunders.

It starts with a few minor instances of permitting ourselves to do what we know is wrong. After all, nobody will find out in the end, so what is the harm? Once we set this moral bar, it's that much easier to take a lackadaisical moral stance and follow similar roads in future, so such choices begin to become our norm.

With each instance, our self-respect diminishes and our relationship with ourselves is degraded. We are gouging our moral base and not repairing it.

When we are old and gray looking back at our lives, do we want to be full of guilt and regret at such decisions—questionable in morals and ethics—we have made throughout life, or do we want to be proud of our convictions? We might be able to amass wealth and external recognition, but our internal worth will be nothing if we have lost our own self-respect. We need to be impeccable in ensuring our actions and words align with our internal moral compass, no matter how hard it is to do so.

What is your relationship with yourself? Do you respect yourself? Do you trust yourself? Can you live with yourself, or do you try to escape your own mind through distractions and external pleasures? Let's start climbing the Summit of Self-Respect.

Authenticity

Throughout my mental health journey, I had to work through an identity dilemma: a disconnect between who I really was and the persona that I thought I needed to portray. I became an actor, adopting a facade based on my perception of who I should be for the particular individuals that I was spending time with. This is not a particularly healthy thing to do, but it's a fairly common coping mechanism, especially for those trying to manage social anxiety. It is often referred to as *character armor* or our *false self*. German phenomenologist Martin Heidegger focused a lot on this human tendency towards inauthenticity, which we adopt in order to conform to the various social roles and societal norms in which we are embedded. Heidegger referred to this concept as *das Man*, which can be translated as *the They* or *One*, as in "the way one behaves." This is our mode of existence when we are choosing our actions, values, thoughts, words, and aspect of life on the basis of our perception of how they should be chosen.

On a societal level, I don't think we've done a very good job at encouraging authenticity. If anything, children are socialized to become whatever is portrayed as acceptable and desirable through the eyes of others. While a degree of socialization is necessary, the media, normative pressures, and celebrity figures often compound unrealistic expectations. The desire to fit in and to embody the image that others, and even we ourselves, have conjured up is a powerful one; we are strongly motivated by real and perceived social responses, as we saw in the Summit of Self-Motivation. The persona that we adopt can be so reinforced and ingrained in our lives that we begin to forget who we really are—the guise takes over instead, and we become a simulation of who we think we should be.

It takes courage and commitment to be ourselves instead of an illusion, but this is a critical component of self-respect. William Shakespeare perhaps said it best in the famous line from *Hamlet*, "This above all: to thine own self be true." Authenticity is about being real and making sure our actions and utterances are in alignment with our true inner beliefs and values. It is a genuine realization and expression of our deepest selves.

Having said all this, there are a few caveats. As we explored in the Summit of Self-Knowledge, our character traits, beliefs, and desires are a complex consequence of our genetic biology combined with the many complex impacts of our upbringing. In this light, we can question how much of the *self* that we are trying to be true to is our *accurate* self and how much is simply a deeper layer that has been instilled in us. What's more, given the way our selves are developed, it is common for us to have undesirable and even callous tendencies and dispositions. So should we be carelessly displaying and acting out these tendencies and character traits in an effort to be fully authentic, or is there an argument for a degree of restraint and integration of learned knowledge in our authenticity?

The goal isn't blind compliance with our innate tendencies. Nor is it that outside influences should be irrelevant. The true goal is to uphold our freedom to choose our thoughts, behaviors, and actions and to display them freely rather than fully succumb to outside influences. We are social creatures, and we need to immerse ourselves in the world around us so we can be informed in our choices and see the degree to which we are maintaining our personal authenticity. I try to be wary of when and how external factors are influencing my thoughts, decisions, and actions, particularly when they manifest themselves as anxiety and embarrassment; this way, I can evaluate my choices more clearly and ensure I'm balancing external considerations with the importance of living out my own authenticity.

Dignity and Respect

Respect is not the same as dignity. Dignity is universal—it is related to our inherent worth as human beings, and we value each other by treating each other with dignity. Respect is not universal; it is earned and lost through actions and deeds.

I have heard people say things like, "Others must respect my opinion!" "I respect everyone!" or "I command respect from my employees." This just isn't how respect works. You may be able to force compliance from employees or demand that others treat you as a dignified human being, but respect has to be earned. When someone is stealing your identity, robbing your house, or abducting your child, are you going to say you respect them? Obviously not. This dilutes and undermines the purpose of the word. That doesn't mean we shouldn't treat people with dignity, including being considerate when it comes to our criticisms and interactions, but claiming respect for everybody regardless of their words and deeds is irresponsible and can often enable further disgraceful actions. If people are not speaking and acting respectfully, they do not earn the respect of others. It is as simple as that. Even parents and other authority figures cannot automatically be treated with unquestioning respect; there are countless examples in which such an assumption of respectability has been disastrous, leading people to overlook political corruption and horrific sex scandals involving religious leaders and other authority figures.

So where do we draw the line?

I think our default position should be to act respectfully towards others and assume they are worthy of a reasonable amount of respect until we have a valid reason not to. This is similar to the "innocent until proven guilty" presumption that all fair and impartial judicial systems are predicated upon. This also extends to the opinions of others. We aren't right all the time, and in order for us to figure out where we are wrong, and more importantly to collectively discover the best paths of action, we need to afford others the respect and dignity required for them to share their views and be heard.

Self-respect is like respect for others. We cannot simply snap our fingers and instantly decide we have a great amount of respect for ourselves. Our level of self-respect is based on our thoughts, behaviors, and actions over time, and we will lose respect for ourselves if we are perpetually thinking and acting in ways we would not respect in others.

Setting the Rules

Establishing and communicating boundaries is essential for maintaining self-respect and self-image, and it is a key component of healthy, long-lasting relationships. If you are going to live with dignity and expect others to respect you, you need to be clear on your boundaries. But before you can draw boundaries, you have to know the terrain. A prerequisite to establishing boundaries is to become more self-aware so that you can understand your feelings and better realize what situations and actions are beyond your level of comfort.

And then it is up to you to set those boundaries and communicate them to others. Without boundaries, you will be more susceptible to others taking advantage of you, so you need to know when to firmly say no, when situations are no longer mentally, emotionally, financially, or physically healthy for you. Boundaries might include behaviors of others that you are unwilling to tolerate or actions asked of you that you are unwilling to carry out. It is best to establish boundaries as early as possible, so that you're not trying to sort things out under pressure or in stressful situations.

If you are an introvert and have friends or coworkers that are particularly extraverted, establishing clear boundaries becomes even more important. Extraverts tend to push personal boundar ies in gregarious and assertive ways that may force introverts to interact in styles that are not comfortable or authentic for them.

Speaking up when you need to say something important is another critical element of self-respect. This is often hard to do, however, since there can be real consequences associated with speaking up. But there are real consequences for remaining silent as well, and the long-term consequences associated with remaining silent often far outweigh the short-term consequences of speaking up. Most of the societal catastrophes that we have seen throughout history were enabled by good people who were too timid to say something when things started to degenerate towards corruption. Small things often go unchallenged and undisputed because people don't want the hassle of having to deal with them. Then the small things compound and become bigger issues. By that point the consequences of speaking up are even more severe, so the silence continues. Eventually, ruin is upon us and it is almost too late: a revolution is needed, or some other drastic measures.

Speaking up doesn't only apply to societal or political issues, however. It is particularly important in relationships to speak up, and do so early, rather than sweeping things under the rug. Having the tough conversations early will prevent issues from bottling up and exploding—at which point the relationship is badly damaged, sometimes irreparably. We are often afraid of hurting another person's feelings, or of the condemnation we will receive from others if the other person says we have hurt their feelings, but it is difficult to discuss anything meaningful or important in life without stirring up substantial feelings on both sides because of how our beliefs become part of us, as we saw in the Summit of Self-Knowledge. If there isn't an emotional sting associated with considering opposing viewpoints, then the topic being discussed probably isn't very meaningful or important to begin with. It is important to maintain a sense of the other person's dignity and the respect they deserve, but that includes respecting them enough to engage with them rather than just disregarding them. Likewise, when someone disagrees with you, however much it upsets you, the forward-thinking thing to do is to deal with it right away, even if it results in conflict. Otherwise, the issues continue to pop up and explode in different forms, over and over again. There is no progress to be found in sticking your head in the sand.

Naturally, it is a lot easier to speak up if we embody the personality traits that support doing so. Unsurprisingly, this means individuals who are high in assertiveness, a subcomponent of extraversion. But everyone has the ability to speak up and needs to exercise this ability, even if it is more difficult and uncomfortable for some. If you find that you have a tough time speaking up, don't simply accept this as a personal failing or limitation. Make it part of your Summit of Self-Respect. There are many quiet voices throughout society that have important things to say but that cannot be heard. Don't be one of these quiet voices. There are ways to develop the skill, and I've talked about some I've used in my own journey in the second chapter, My Internal Everest.

Responsibility

Self-respect has past, present, and future considerations. Let's look at the future first—specifically responsibility, which is about taking ownership of what happens to us going forward.

Although rights are important for us to maintain and protect, what we often conveniently overlook is the importance of balancing rights with responsibility, which really go hand-in-hand. In the same way that freedom can soon be taken away if citizens don't collectively keep tyranny at bay, the cost of maintaining rights is paid for through adopting responsibility. This can be a sobering realization.

Adopting personal responsibility throughout our lives is probably the most important decision we can make. It has far-reaching mental, physical, and emotional benefits. It is not extraordinarily difficult to take responsibly for our lives, but it often seems easier not to, which is why the adoption of personal responsibility is relatively rare in our society.

Responsibility is not a single action; it represents an approach to thinking and living founded on the belief that success and failure are largely within our own control. This isn't to say we don't all have unique challenges, some more extreme than others, as we've been exploring, but it is to say that our own decisions and actions play a critical role in what happens to us.

The opposite of responsibility is obviously irresponsibility, but there are many different ways we can be irresponsible. In the context of self-respect, I want to focus on a particularly concerning mentality that is the sworn enemy of personal responsibility: *entitlement.* Entitlement is the expectation of favorable conditions and favorable treatment and a sense that these are deserved based on existence or circumstances. Under the guise of entitlement, favorable outcomes do not have to be earned, they are owed—and the response is angry pouting or chaotic retaliation when they are not met.

From a psychology perspective, a sense of entitlement is usually associated with a high level of narcissism: an inflated sense of one's own importance. If you are particularly interested in understanding narcissism, Robert Raskin and Calvin Hall developed a tool in 1979 that is used widely by researchers and for hiring purposes, known as the Narcissistic Personality Inventory (NPI). For our purposes, however, it is important to realize that there are two types of narcissistic tendencies. The first is grandiose narcissism, which is an unrealistic sense of superiority and dominance that is generally correlated with high extraversion and low neuroticism. The second is vulnerable narcissism, which is characterized by insecurity and excessive self-absorption and is generally correlated with low extraversion and high neuroticism. A certain level of concern and admiration for oneself is healthy, as we have already discussed, but like most things that need to remain in balance, this can be taken way too far. Narcissists have a deep need for excessive attention and admiration while lacking any empathy for others. They feel the world revolves around them.

The narcissistic tendencies that result in a sense of entitlement are partially inherited genetically but seem to be linked most closely with parent-child relationships. Parents that swoop in to give their children whatever they want often produce entitled children through excessive adoration and continuously giving in to requests throughout childhood. On the other end of the spectrum, excessive criticism and neglect in child rearing also seems to lead to a sense of entitlement. Broken families and busier lifestyles result in less time and attention given to raising children, which seems to be a major factor in the development of an entitled mentality.

I worked for a few years as a college professor as I was transitioning out of engineering into my current vocation, and during that time I noticed an elevated sense of entitlement among my students. There was an underlying expectation that they should pass simply for showing up, and the college policies seem to have exacerbated this expectation. Department funding depended on students moving on to the next year, so assignments, group projects, and exams were simplified to what I felt was an unacceptable level. I was teaching technical subjects where many of my students would end up in manufacturing, nuclear, and engineering jobs, and failure to understand and apply the basic concepts could easily result in disasters and fatalities.

I taught approximately 110 students each semester, and even with such lenient requirements, I would still end up having to give between 5 and 10 percent of them a failing grade. These were students that didn't show up to the exams, didn't hand in their term papers, showed up to class drunk or high, drew cartoons on their test papers, and other such disappointments. I found out, though, that even for those students, the college then had "promotional meetings" where the administrators and full-time staff got together and tried to figure out how they could adjust their grade distributions in order to justify passing them anyways. From a psychological perspective, the most concerning aspect wasn't so much the ethical considerations of doing this, it was its effect on the mentalities of the students. Many of my students knew that they would be passed in the end, and it affected their attitudes and commitment towards their work: they felt entitled to be passed to the next year just because they were enrolled—they were the "client" or "customer," and the customer is always right.

And yet, despite the learning landscape, I also had some students who were very responsible and went above and beyond expectations, doing everything they could to maximize their future chances of success. These students lifted my spirits and reinforced my belief in everyone's ability to choose a responsible route, regardless of the environmental conditions.

You will be in many situations like this throughout your life, where the structural and societal support is not ideal and there are opportunities—even encouragement—to take the expedient and easy route. Instead, take things into your own hands and decide that you are going to assume responsibility for improving yourself and your situation, regardless of your external circumstances. You will respect yourself—and you will also improve yourself.

The Victim Mentality

Related to entitlement and narcissism is the victim mentality, a dysfunctional mindset whereby a person incessantly feels the world is out to get them and bring them down. It is a personality disorder that is sometimes also referred to as victim syndrome, victim complex, or victim identity. There are three underlying beliefs that are embraced by those who have succumbed to the victim mentality. The first is the belief that their lives are exceedingly difficult and that bad things always happen to them. The second is that such personal misfortune is the fault of other people and of circumstances out of their own control. The third is that any attempt to make things better will certainly fail, so it is better to not even try.

It is important to distinguish the victim mentality from the temporary feelings of sympathy, self-pity, or grief that most everyone feels when fate deals an unfortunate blow. These transitory bouts of sorrow and heartache are a natural part of being human. It is also important to distinguish the victim mentality from true victimization. When real damage is being done in the form of tyranny, persecution, harassment, physical harm, and other blatant maltreatments, these are valid reasons for concern that need to be addressed head-on with consequences for the guilty parties. These types of harmful events, especially in childhood, can contribute to the development of a victim mentality later in life, and individuals who have been victimized tend to have a negativity bias just as those with victim mentality do. But the key differentiator is that the victim mentality generalizes to a belief in unconditional and perpetual victimhood throughout life, even in the absence of any evidence of present harm.

A person with a victim mentality allows it to define them, so deep down there is a part of them that doesn't want to let it go. They will complain that nobody is helping them, but then they will push help away, since improvement would reduce justification and external sympathy. Conversations are full of drama in an effort to make others feel sorry for them, but they often respond in passive-aggressive ways to anyone trying to help. Probably the most significant reason why individuals cling to the victim mentality is that it allows them to avoid the burden of assuming personal responsibility. This is what is known psychologically as *secondary gain*. Secondary gains may include increased attention, medication, remuneration, justification for frequently missing work, abdicating responsibility for care of dependents, dodging school, not having to show up on time, avoiding punishments, and similar subconsciously perceived benefits.

There is a strangely alluring and oddly satisfying response associated with victimhood. If your life is falling apart, adopting a sense of victimhood is a type of survival mechanism. By finding someone or something to blame for everything bad that is happening, you can have the relative "pleasure" of avoiding a degree of personal pain—the pain of having nobody or nothing to blame but one's own actions and inactions. If I'm being honest with myself, I've experienced this odd satisfaction at times in my own life when I've allowed myself to feel like a victim.

One of my friends from childhood followed a series of paths of destruction that have led him to the point of rock bottom many times over. We used to drink and get into all sorts of trouble when we were young, but he never seemed to mature and grow out of it. He's experienced everything from jail terms and lawsuits to alcoholism, drugs, and sleeping in alleyways—every time I think he can't possibly sink to new lows, he seems to find a way. One of the last times we got together, he was living with some other homeless individuals on the edge of a marsh, so I met him there, and we went for a long walk. As we walked, he told me about how things were just stacked up against him, and he said that every time things would start getting better for him, he felt a force pulling him away from the path of recovery he was on and driving him to screw it all up again. He signaled to his head with his hand tensed in a claw shape, as though there were a demon that would grab his mind and pull him back down.

And that's what it looks like from the outside: his life has been a series of small upward pushes followed by steep declines through various forms of self-sabotage, over and over again. His predisposition to such behavior is complex and childhood traumas cannot be disregarded, as we've already explored, but the demon you see pulling him down is within him. He is the victim and the victimizer. He has received various forms of help from compassionate individuals over the years, but one by one he eventually pushes them away. He had a boss that was helping him out for a while, but his boss could only handle so much of the alcoholic tendencies and drama, so eventually the second chances ran out. A similar scenario played itself out with his girlfriend, with whom he had a child and can tragically not visit anymore.

Your life is almost certainly not much like his. But is it a little like it, in any small way? If you have your own mental health challenges in particular, ask yourself honestly: Is there a part of you that is holding on to your mental health challenges as a crutch or an excuse for avoiding actions that you should be taking? This is a painful notion that your mind may immediately try to write off as foolish, but it is not uncommon for there to be a part of you that doesn't want to let go of that with which you have been identified. But you need to let it go. It isn't worth the long-term damage, and you deserve to be free of it. You don't have to go through the journey alone if you are finding it impossible to do so. Get the support you need, but remember: It is you who has to make the decision and initiate the process and stick with it.

Adam's Journey

My older brother Adam's educational journey is an inspiring positive example of the importance of adopting responsibility for one's own future.

When Adam was in elementary school, he didn't fit in. He was easily distracted, even in kindergarten, and he learned differently than the other kids, so he wasn't receiving much help in the classroom. By the time he was in third grade, he ended up in front of a panel of his teachers, the principal, and the school psychologist, where they diagnosed him with a learning disability and the label attention deficit disorder (ADD).

Labeling is not without its justifications. We need specificity in approaching challenges, and to some extent this kind of identification has its roots in an increased understanding of child and adolescent challenges. But when we are given labels, they can easily become defining factors that shape our futures. Common labels like "disruptive," "hyperactive," "troublemaker," "artistic," "athletic," "problem child," or "math genius" stick with people and influence their decisions. They become self-fulfilling prophesies and provide us with a justification that we can pin all of our shortcomings on, rather than working through them. I experienced this at first when I was told I had an anxiety disorder: it caused me to concentrate more and more on the aspects of my life that were influenced by, or a result of, the disorder I had been labeled with. In my brother's case, he was moved to a special education class with only eight other students and had a difficult journey through elementary school and most of high school, relying on the teachers and school system to determine his trajectory in life. My parents were worried about whether he would even be able to graduate high school.

But in twelfth grade, Adam decided that he wasn't going to continue relying on others. He was going to take responsibility for his own future.

He seemed to have a flair for electronics, so the first thing he enrolled in was a programming class, which he excelled at. With his programming marks, he received the President's Scholarship to attend college for a short while so he could finish the math and physics prerequisites he had missed in high school. This allowed him to apply to university, where he chose engineering.

He was accepted and after his first year decided to pursue electrical engineering, one of the most difficult and mathematically intense disciplines. He now works as a professional engineer and is truly brilliant in the way he can spatially visualize solutions multiple steps ahead.

My mother played a significant role in advocating for Adam along his journey, but more than anything it was his own decision to take responsibility. With that commitment, he was focused on solutions rather than problems; he discovered how he learned, and he ended up completing one of the most difficult university degrees to achieve.

I've shared Adam's story for two reasons. The first is as a caution about labeling people. Not everyone is able to overcome their labels and arrive at the same success that my brother had. Many people are paralyzed by the labels they are given, to the point where they give up on striving and succumb to the whims of the world around them. But the second and more purposeful reason is to drive home the importance of adopting responsibility, and the positive changes this decision can make in our lives. In my view, a commitment to responsibility is one of the most important mentality changes we can make for our futures. And if you are a parent, the sooner you can encourage your children to start taking responsibility, the better they will be equipped to play a positive and productive role in society.

Initiating Change

One last area where I believe responsibility is critically important is when it comes to initiating change. Too commonly, we sit around waiting for things to change. Sometimes fate shines down on us and things change in our favor, but this doesn't happen very often. If we want things to change, the proactive thing to do is to take responsibility and get involved in initiating the change. This applies to external situations, but perhaps even more importantly, this applies to initiating internal change in our minds.

A good family friend of ours used to be a pipe smoker, a habit and addiction he had picked up from his father. He had struggled on and off with trying to quit for a lot of years but, as those who have struggled with addiction can attest, quitting can be immensely difficult. About ten years ago, though, he decided that enough was enough. His pipe smoking was a problem that mattered to him, it was something he was able to influence, and if he wanted to make positive changes in his life, it was his responsibility to make it happen. He gathered up all the tobacco pipes his father had given him and broke each one of them into tiny pieces so they were no longer usable. He was also a fairly heavy drinker, and he took a similar course of action to eliminate alcohol from his life—symbolic actions that were part of his deeper personal commitment to succeed. Taking responsibility for the health of his future self wasn't easy, but he is now happier and healthier than ever before. Not only that, he has the personal satisfaction that such lifestyle changes are possible and that he had the willpower to bring them to fruition.

I really do believe responsibility is a choice. Most people who perpetually fail at taking responsibility and bringing about change are quick to point out all the outward factors that make it "impossible." These factors are real, and some people have it much harder than others, but it simply isn't helpful to continue blaming outward circumstances and using them as excuses for avoiding taking responsibility. Climbing mountains takes many steps and much time, and the bigger the mountain, the more steps and the more days and the more obstacles there are. But you still have to start by taking a step, and another, and another, and however far you get, you are farther than you were.

Integrity

While responsibility is all about taking ownership for our future selves, integrity refers to our thoughts and actions in the present—the here and now. Integrity is our word of honor, our ethical convictions, and our adherence to deep moral principles.

The word *integrity* is derived from the Latin for integrating or bringing together. Integrity is the psychological integration of our inner morality with our outer reality. It is the consistency in which we carry out what is right. There is an element of wholeness to integrity, which is why we feel distress when we act in ways that contradict our deep moral compass. Integrity is not the part of us that is influenced by the reaction or acknowledgment of others. It is the part of us that is constrained to do the right thing in the absence of social feedback and regardless of our shallower desires.

I touched on some of the concepts of integrity in the Summit of Self-Motivation, when we discussed the internal motivator of personal value conformance. We are motivated to maintain our integrity, but we often have conflicting motivators as well, which is why our integrity often doesn't prevail.

Integrity is correlated positively with agreeableness and conscientiousness. The correlations are relatively weak, however, which is why some researchers have suggested integrity should be a personality factor of its own—for example, Kibeom Lee and Michael Ashton developed the HEXACO Personality Inventory, which adds a sixth factor, that of honesty-humility, to the Big Five. Like the other traits we have been exploring, there is a genetic aspect and a nurture aspect associated with integrity, but how integrity is modeled throughout our upbringing seems to play a particularly important role.

Naturally, we might then ask, "Is there anything more to integrity than playing out the predetermined programming from our nature and our nurturing?" If you take a deterministic viewpoint, then any perceived choice we have when it comes to maintaining our integrity—or any other perceived choice, for that matter—is an illusion. Our scientific models tend to be limited to a deterministic explanation, so naturally the data we have support it because they're based on it, but there are countless aspects of human consciousness that we haven't been able to model and don't understand in the least. In real life, we always act as though we have free will—and, as we saw in the Summit of Self-Balance, "Whether you think you can, or you think you can't, you're right." It is my belief that each of us has free will, and we are able to make choices independent of our preconditioned conditions and constraints, but even if I am wrong, this is how we behave and this is how we treat each other.

When it comes to integrity, we are often faced with choices between what is right and what is convenient. Integrity is about choosing to do what is right, which highly influences and determines our degree of self-respect. We can either choose to maintain our self-respect or choose cheap personal gains or avoidance of small losses, such as a damaged ski repair charge— at the expense of our self-respect.

Having a deep sense of integrity is relatively rare. It is a quality, though, that is looked up to, especially when it comes to leadership. A lot of things are transient throughout life: success, friends, relationships, money, enemies, happiness, hairstyles... Integrity is something that you can commit to that will last forever. It is the bedrock that will support you through much of the chaotic uncertainty of life. True, you aren't going to be able to live a life of complete and flawless integrity; even when you have the best of intentions, there will be times when you slip and you stumble. But there is really no better aim that will guide your decisions and actions throughout life. Learn from each time you fail to uphold your integrity, and better yourself each time so that you can take the high road the next time you are faced with similar decisions. A life of integrity is something you can and should look back on with pride and satisfaction.

The Four-Way Test

How, specifically, can we train ourselves in integrity? One way is The Four-Way Test.

I am a member of an international service organization called Rotary, which is a global network of clubs that carry out local and global philanthropy projects. When I became a Rotarian, I was given a small plaque that I have hanging in my office. It is known as *The Four-Way Test of the things we think, say or do*. Originally authored by Herbert Taylor in 1932, it is a litmus test that Rotarians are encouraged to think about when conducting business, and more broadly in our personal and professional lives:

1   Is it the truth?
2   Is it fair to all concerned?
3   Will it build goodwill and better friendships?
4   Will it be beneficial to all concerned?

It is a bit of a paradox that it is written on a reference plaque, since true integrity comes from deep within, but more than anything it is a reminder of the importance of maintaining our integrity. It is sometimes helpful to have a reference blueprint for self-reflection in order to add some structure to the way we evaluate decisions and actions. Although it is an external reference, I think it is a good start in the types of questions we need to continuously ask ourselves when making decisions, communicating with others, making professional transactions, and in all other areas of our lives.

The first point in particular is important: "Is it the truth?"

Albert Einstein's belief was that "whoever is careless with the truth in small matters cannot be trusted with important matters," and my own experience has shown me that there is a lot of wisdom in this statement. People who tout the innocence of their habitual "little white lies" seem to take a similar moral stance when it comes to speaking the truth on critical issues. In the same way that you can usually get a good feel for the character of person by how they treat the hotel clerk, you can get a good feel for a person's overall honesty by how transparent and honest they are with small details.

Lying is often a protection mechanism to begin with. We want to protect our image, our resources, our opportunities, our friends, our money, or our family, for example. It is embarrassing and painful when we compromise or lose these things, so the expedient thing to do in the moment is often to lie to protect— to sidestep the perceived immediate consequences associated with the truth. In the long run, however, it is detrimental not only to our relationships, but ultimately to ourselves. It erodes our self-worth and self-respect, one "little white lie" at a time. It also diverts a lot of mental energy and focus because of the compounding effect required to maintain a lie: we not only have to remember our lies, we have to constantly create other lies to corroborate and defend the fabrication. Perhaps most detrimentally, though, lying demotivates us from actually becoming or achieving in reality the contents and achievements that are propped up by our lies in the first place.

If you want to have self-respect, speaking the truth is an essential commitment to make in all aspects of life. Say what you are going to do, and then do what you have said. This is the foundation for living with honesty and integrity. Firm footings like this also attract and encourage more truth from those around you. Strive to become an example you can be proud of, and surround yourself with similar individuals committed to truth.

Accountability

While integrity refers to how we conduct our lives in the present, accountability is how we develop and maintain our self-respect for past actions. Accountability is very much related to responsibility, in that the accountability we accept for past decisions and actions becomes our responsibility for making future amends. *Accountability* stems from the word *account*, and it means being able to provide an account of our results—in other words, being answerable for our actions.

My father-in-law has a farm, and one day a number of years ago he was planting corn in the field when he saw a large moving truck stop by the side of the road. The driver hopped out, walked around to the back of the truck, and started pulling bags of garbage out and throwing them in the ditch in front of the farm. By the time the man was finished dumping the garbage, my father-in-law was just close enough that he was able to catch the name of the moving company that was printed on the side of the truck before it pulled away.

He was annoyed, not only because of how ill-mannered this was but because now he would have to get rid of the garbage himself. Before he did so, however, he went home and called the moving company. He ended up speaking with the owner, who was shocked to hear about the incident and promised to look into it right away. A little while later, he received a call back from the owner explaining that he had identified the perpetrator and was sending him back to pick up the garbage, on his own time, in a manner that would satisfy both the owner and my father-in-law.

The truck driver arrived at the front door later in the day and sheepishly said he had picked up all the garbage. He then asked if my father-in-law would call his boss back right away, since his boss had said he wouldn't be paid until my father-in-law was satisfied with the clean-up job. My father-in-law said he would be happy to call the boss back once he inspected the area where the garbage was, so the two of them did a quick walk-around. Everything looked fine, so the boss was called and the driver went on his way. He kept his job because of his quick action to make things right.

I quite enjoyed hearing about how this incident turned out. If only every culprit was held accountable for their deeds in this way, the world would be a much better place! Obviously, there are laws, enforcement officers, and judges that hold all of us accountable to some degree for our actions. But I'm less interested in that type of accountability than I am in personal accountability.

In 2002, Steven Spielberg released the film *Catch Me if You Can*, loosely based on the biography and fraudulent escapades of Frank Abagnale Jr. It is an exciting film about how Frank posed as a pilot, a doctor, and an attorney while forging millions of dollars' worth of phony checks. Frank was just a teenager when he started, and it took the FBI and other law enforcement agencies around the world years to finally catch him. He was eventually sent to prison, but a few years into serving his sentence, the FBI released him—on the condition that he help the agency investigate fraud and scam artists.

Although the movie is entertaining, what I found most intriguing was when I read more about the real Frank Abagnale Jr.'s adult life. He felt a duty to repay his wrongdoings and ended up working with the FBI for decades. He was offered three pardons from three different presidents and refused them all. He doesn't believe a piece of paper will excuse what he did; only through his actions can he attempt to make amends.

I don't know all the details of Frank's life, but I admire the way that he has held himself accountable for his past actions and has taken it upon himself to do what he can to make things right. This strikes me as an inspiring example of personal accountability. Personal accountability is the conviction that we are fully accountable for the consequences of our actions. It is not about beating ourselves up or dwelling on regrets. Instead, it is a mindset and a conscious decision to accept the reality of our past actions and take ownership for the results. This is the summit we are climbing, each of us on our own: adopting a sense of ownership for ourselves, for good and bad outcomes and the resulting consequences. Ultimately, this is the antidote to the victim mentality.

ACTIONS AND BEHAVIORS	SELF-TALK AND DIALOGUE
• Take ownership	• "I won't stand by"
• Focus on solutions	• "What can I do?"
• Embrace challenges and change	• "I can do it!"
• Approach proactively	• "I will make it better"
• Accept reality	• "It's on me"
• Seek constructive feedback	• "Life has ups and downs"
	• "I can"

ACCOUNTABLE MENTALITY

VICTIM MENTALITY

• Blame society and others	• "Not my problem to fix"
• Make excuses	• "Life is against me"
• Focus on problems	• "Who can I blame?"
• Complain about everything	• "Everyone else has it better than me"
• Deny reality	• "Why would I even try?"
• Wait and hope for others to fix things	• "Not me"
• Abdicate responsibility	• "I can't"
• Approach reactively	• "The world is out to get me"

Look Inward

The first step to becoming more self-accountable is to habitually practice looking inward at yourself rather than looking outward to see who else should be held accountable. This is a hard thing to do, especially if you are used to looking outside of yourself. It requires a firm decision that you are in control and that you are the one who has to experience the consequences and rewards associated with what your actions and inactions bring about.

Recognizing inaction is critical. When disaster happens, the temptation is to conclude that nothing you did could have contributed to it. But you have to consider the things you should have done but didn't. This is a hard pill to swallow, but it is important, and if you dig deep you can always identify early warning signs that you ignored or failed to act upon. Learn from these realizations.

The next part of accountability is to understand the intricacies around why you are taking action or deciding not to take action to begin with. This is where the introspection strategies we explored in the Summit of Self-Knowledge are important. It is difficult to hold yourself accountable if you are missing pieces of the story or acting out someone else's aspirations instead of your own. You need to believe in what you are doing if you expect to feel a sense of ownership for the outcomes.

I have personally found that putting together a plan and being very clear on what the acceptable outcomes need to be has been very helpful in holding myself accountable. My clarity in the outcomes is actually more important than my plan, since I frequently adjust my plan as I learn from mistakes and successes along the way. If I am vague on my success criteria, however, or I don't have any of the steps hashed out for getting there, it is easier to just let things slide after the fact. When I end up with lukewarm results in the end, I can brush them off as no big deal since I didn't have a sharp vision to begin with. The clearer you can be with your envisioned plan and results, the more accountable you will be for any outcome.

Lastly, rewarding and disciplining yourself, even subtly, is an excellent way to hold yourself accountable. You need to hold yourself to whatever criteria you establish, though, or you'll simply erode your accountability for future actions. Obviously, you should be careful about drastic self-discipline, as we covered in the Summit of Self-Balance, since you don't want to be beating yourself up, but you do want to learn something in the process. Remember, the goal is self-improvement and learning, not mistreatment and self-abuse, so be kind to yourself in the process. Reward and discipline yourself in the same way that you would reward and discipline a loved one.

Strengthen Your Autobiography

Imagine you are writing your autobiography and including all the details of your life that only you know about. I have used this as a mental litmus test in terms of maintaining my own self-respect. Would I be proud to read about myself?

Ask yourself this same question: Would you be proud of your own autobiography?

You can't change the past, but even if you are in a deep valley, you can climb towards a peak if you start now. Your ability to change your future is within your grasp. Your past shortcomings set you up for the perfect success story that will inspire others. You can't walk away from yourself, so you might as well become the type of person you want to stick with and can rely on for always doing what is right. Your autobiography is only partially written at this point in your life. Make the ending a narrative you will feel great about reading.

Expedition Debrief

As I have said a few times before, the key is to start where you are now and focus on what you can do from this point forward. Don't dwell on past moral failings; you cannot change the past, but you can make up for previous blunders by pragmatically altering your thinking and actions. Take inventory of yourself as you are now. Do you respect yourself?

Do you often stay silent when you have something important to say? Make a personal commitment going forward to speak up, even if you have to face certain consequences. Remember that there are long-term consequences to remaining silent that often far outweigh the short-term consequences of speaking up.

Remember the principles of responsibility, integrity, and accountably that we have explored. All three are vitally important to truly respecting and honoring yourself. Take responsibility for your future, live with integrity, and be accountable for your actions. This is the path less traveled, but it is also the path to absolute self-respect.

Above all, guard yourself against the victim mentality! It is such a tempting and oddly satisfying mental state, but there is nothing good at the end of that road. Are there aspects of your life where you are clinging to blame and resentment and subconsciously are unwilling to move on? Let them go. Take responsibility for your life and adopt a realistic and optimistic belief in your own ability to craft your future. That is the only route to self-respect and improving your life.

There may appear to be shortcuts to the summit when it comes to self-respect, but don't be lured down them—they may seem viable, but they ultimately loop around and you'll end up back where you currently are, or sometimes even lower down on the mountain. Stick to the tough but upward-leading path of truth, fairness, and integrity, and you'll find yourself headed towards the Summit of Self-Respect.

THE SUMMIT OF SELF-RESILIENCE

South Face of Everest

The area above 26,000 feet (7,925 meters) on Everest is known as the death zone, and for good reason. The available oxygen is so limited at that altitude that human cells die at an accelerated rate and the natural regeneration of cells stops. Strength and motor function deteriorate rapidly, neurological dysfunction impairs judgment to the point of delirium, blood circulation to extremities decreases, digestion slows almost to a halt, and minute by minute the human body degenerates towards unconsciousness. In a desperate attempt to endure, our body's natural survival mechanisms suppress non-essential bodily functions in favor of diverting blood to vital organs. These survival efforts may temporarily delay the inevitable, but if you stay too long in the death zone, you will die. The year my family and I were attempting Everest, three people had already passed away in the death zone before we got that far. Hearing about their deaths was a chilling reminder of the fragility of human life and the importance of taking such an expedition very seriously.

We had spent nearly eight hours climbing from Camp 3 and had only been at Camp 4 a few hours to replenish our water supplies when we headed out again that same night on our summit attempt. Since Camp 4 is in the death zone, spending additional time there in an effort to rest and recover is futile. We were using supplemental oxygen at that point to preserve our energy for higher up, although the flow rate was low to ensure we didn't prematurely run out. It was pitch black when we turned our backs on the camp and headed out towards the steep South Face of Everest. The dim glow of our headlamps provided barely adequate visibility to find the route, but we were able to use the shreds of tattered ropes that had been used by past expeditions as a guide.

After a few hours of climbing, blowing snow began to sweep across our path, and soon we were in a full-on blizzard. The worst part was that the blowing snow would cake itself to the outside of the fixed climbing ropes that had been anchored along the steepest sections. We were using mechanical ascenders that had a little cam in them with teeth, which were designed to slide freely in one direction on the ropes but then lock when we would put our weight against them or slip backward. But the snow on the ropes would fill in the little teeth of the cam and turn to ice, voiding their gripping ability. There were a number of times when the crampons on my mountaineering boots slipped on exposed rocks and my ascender failed to stop my fall. I ended up in a rapid descent down the icy slope, desperately grasping at the rocks, ice chunks, and any rope shreds I could get hold of.

That climb through the night ended up being one of the most demanding and harrowing aspects of the expedition. What made it especially arduous was the culmination of so many challenges all at once. In addition to physical exhaustion from the climbing we had completed during the day, my lack of sleep was taking a heavy toll on my abilities. I was also still quite ill from exposure to sicknesses at Base Camp and the altitude's weakening of my immune system. Ice had formed on the inside of my goggles, and the oxygen mask I was using kept freezing up from the moisture in my breath, to the point where I would have to continually squeeze it to break up the ice. The slope of the icy face we were climbing approached vertical in some sections, and the bitter wind and blowing snow were relentless. To top it all off, the visibility afforded me by my small headlamp was insufficient to the point that I kept having to remove my googles to try to see what I was doing and where I was going, risking eye damage from the harsh cold. The failure of my ascender was almost the last straw. I remember shakily grasping to the ropes with both hands, having just been able to pull myself out of a downward slide, and thinking, "What else could this mountain possibly throw at us?"

It was times like that where resilience was particularly important. As much as the challenges continued to present themselves, one upon the next, I had to take a deep breath and realize that despite the precarious reality I was faced with, I needed to find a way to pick myself back up and continue on.

Taking off my mountaineering glove, I scratched away at the ice built up on the teeth of the ascender cam with my fingernail until the teeth were once again visible. Then I clipped the ascender onto the nearest rope and continued putting one foot in front of the other. That falling sequence followed by scratching away at the ice occurred many times, and the other challenges didn't go away either, but I was inching my way forward in spite of it all.

What Is Resilience?

The word *resilience* is derived from the Latin *resilire*, which means to rebound or recoil. It was originally used primarily in material science and engineering to describe the ability of materials to absorb energy and deform elastically without succumbing to failure and to release that energy upon returning to their original form. A similar concept later evolved figuratively to apply to living beings that could rebound and recover quickly after facing significant adversity, trauma, stress, or crisis.

Human beings have four main types of resilience: physical, mental, emotional, and social—social resilience being a community's or group's ability to cope with and respond to challenges. Although all of these are important, in this chapter we will be focusing primarily on mental and emotional resilience. This is what is generally referred to as self-resilience or psychological resilience. It's our ability to adapt well to adversity and return to pre-crisis status relatively quickly and unscathed.

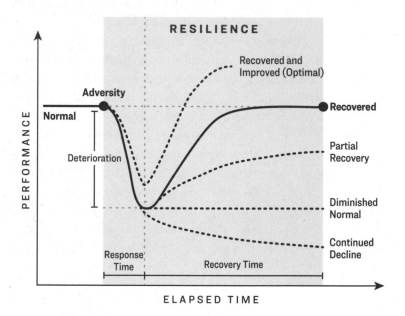

Our scientific understanding of resilience has evolved significantly over the last hundred years. It is a complex topic, and there is still much we don't understand, but each new discovery provides us with the possibility to better equip ourselves for the next precipitous ridge we face on our journey. Much of the earliest inquiry and understanding of resilience was highly focused on individual traits, qualities, and heritable characteristics. The understanding then evolved to focus on environmental risk factors and protective factors that predispose individuals to vulnerability and affect people's potential to acquire resilient qualities. Over the last few decades, our understanding of resilience has taken a positive psychology perspective focusing on optimism, motivation, the development of internal strength, and psychological growth through transcendence of adversity.

There are benefits in all three of these eras of research and understanding, but I am particularly optimistic about the latest discoveries in the nature of resilience because they align with my own perspective: Although we all have unique challenges, we are not simply victims of circumstance and biological heritage. We can and should consciously and deliberately take steps to influence our destiny.

The reason resilience is so important is that life is full of volatile and ever-changing circumstances that cut deep into even our most well-established and well-rehearsed plans. The hard truth is that nothing in the physical world is permanent or unshakable, and the foundations that we rely on and take for granted can dissolve under us at any moment.

Resilience doesn't shield us from emotional pain or the sense of loss and hurt that follows tragedy, but it allows us to work through grief and recover in a timely manner. When we experience the loss of a loved one, a diagnosis of serious illness, job loss, failed relationships, or other potentially devastating life events, it is resilience that enables us to remain level-headed and continue to function. In essence, the stability that resilience brings helps prevent things from getting even worse. Even when it comes to less-extreme day-to-day stressors, resilience helps us remain balanced and shields us from getting too overwhelmed. Setbacks are inevitable in our fast-paced lives, but resilient individuals tend to flourish and rebound stronger and better prepared.

Who Is More Likely to Be Resilient?

Human beings in general are quite resilient, but there is a lot of variation in the way people respond to setbacks, and there are many different factors affecting that. Resilience can be seen as both a character trait and a skill set, in that there are immutable components associated with our genetics, but it is also something that can be practiced and learned. Resilience is negatively correlated with neuroticism—meaning individuals high in neuroticism are generally not as resilient—and positively correlated with the other four traits, extraversion and conscientiousness being the strongest predictors. Various neurobiological studies have also correlated self-resilience with specific genes and neurochemical levels, particularly serotonin and dopamine, as well as differing neural circuits and pathways between individuals.

We have much more established findings when it comes to the social, parental, and environmental factors that influence resilience capacity. Environmental risk factors include low socioeconomic status, excessive family conflict, neglect, parental and sibling drug abuse, ineffectual discipline or maltreatment, poverty, antisocial values, lack of support resources, and physical, verbal or sexual abuse. Environmental protective factors, on the other hand, include supportive role models, good parenting, pro-social values, well-defined roles and responsibilities, trusting relationships, community belonging, parental attention and attachment, a healthy social network, and access to support resources.

The solution may look simple: increase our protective factors and decrease our risk factors. But this is easier said than done since these factors are embedded in the fabric of our sociocultural and familial structures. And so these findings can be disheartening because such environmental factors are largely, if not entirely, out of our control when we are children and adolescents. Focusing on them encourages a deterministic acceptance of the outcomes—it gives us excuses and justifications for lack of self-resilience—which isn't particularly helpful from a practical perspective looking forward.

The question has to be asked: to what extent is it society's responsibility—and ability—to ameliorate my risk factors, and to what extent is it my own? Some individuals are able to show tremendous resilience despite being in the high-risk category, and some individuals with very little risk cannot cope with even minimal adversity. We need more comprehensive models and understandings of the many internal and external processes beyond environmental factors. And we need to take a forward-looking approach: as with most of what I recommend in this book, I prefer to focus on what you can do from where you are right now to make meaningful improvements.

The fact is that resilience is deeply ingrained within us, to the point where it isn't easy to pinpoint exactly what has made us resilient or what has contributed to our lack of resilience. It all interacts and works together. And so a holistic approach is warranted, and by improving other areas of our lives, we generally also improve our resilience. In fact, much of our training and experience on the other summits—including self-awareness, emotional regulation, and self-motivation—gives us strategies and skillsets that also help us become more resilient. The key is to recognize where we are lacking and to commit to taking small steps to improve ourselves in these areas.

There are, however, some specific strategies that I would like to share that I think are particularly effective in building up our resilience, ideally in conjunction with what we have already covered. These strategies are a bit like practicing for a mountaineering expedition by climbing some of the steep hills around your community. The two endeavors aren't quite the same thing, but there are transferable aspects that can help a person to be better prepared.

Tap into Your Motivation Strategies

The relationship between resilience and motivation is complex. In the simplest view, it takes a degree of motivation in order to be resilient. But there are many individuals who are highly motivated but lack the resilience needed to adapt and bounce back when faced with hardships. If you recall from the Summit of Self-Motivation, motivation is our inner drive or urge to take action, but it is not necessarily as strong in the face of setbacks and unexpected challenges. In some sense, resilience can be thought of an augmentation of motivation—or the phenomenon that enables motivation to prevail against time and adversity.

Because of the relationship between resilience and motivation, a first strategy in bolstering your resilience can be to refer back to some of the concepts we explored relating to motivation, as many are transferable. I have personally found the self-talk and social accountability strategies we explored earlier to be beneficial in giving me the extra boost needed to pick myself back up when I've been knocked down by adverse occurrences.

Consistency

One of the most important things to remember when it comes to strengthening your resilience is consistency, even when it comes to seemingly inconsequential things. Resilience can be thought of a little bit like a muscle, in that it has to be exercised frequently if you hope to have the strength in place when it really matters. If you are not able to flex your resilience muscle when it comes to the small things, how can you hope to have a chance when it comes to more important challenges? You can also think of resilience in the habitual sense, in that the more you make it a habit to bounce back quickly, the more it becomes second nature to do so. It becomes easier the more it is ingrained in your daily life, and small successes bring about the positivity needed to continue the trend.

I am very careful with my internal dialogue and internal commitments for this reason. If I make a commitment to myself to read for one hour a day for one week straight, you could say that it doesn't matter much if I don't keep the commitment because other things come up, and on the surface this is true, but each time I fail to get myself back on track, I incrementally erode my own resilience. The classic New Year's resolutions are an excellent example of this. Every year millions of people set goals for themselves to adopt workout schedules, lose weight, quit smoking, quit drinking, find a new job, etcetera. As the days and weeks pass, other temptations and priorities get in the way, and the vast majority of New Year's resolutions are abandoned.

Be careful with even the smallest challenges you commit to, as the way you respond to adversity in small things will mold and influence the way you respond in much more distressing and consequential circumstances.

Insert the "Yet"

I have noticed that what seems to separate resilient people from those who give up at the first sign of trouble is a mentality shift that recognizes our innate ability to improve with each try. Remember that Thomas Edison reportedly failed ten thousand times before perfecting the incandescent light bulb. Many of us, faced with such insistent failure, will have thoughts such as "I can't figure this out," "I'm not good enough," or "I just don't have the experience." But resilient people say to themselves, "I can't figure this out *yet*," "I'm not good enough *yet*," or "I just don't have the experience *yet*," and then they set about getting themselves to a stage where they will be successful.

And so that is a strategy that I have found to be beneficial for building resilience: to insert the word *yet* into my internal thoughts, and even into my external dialogue when applicable, when dealing with lack of success. When you change your internal dialogue, you begin to view failures more like temporary setbacks rather than catastrophic show-stoppers.

Find the Funny

A few years ago I was booked to speak at a conference, and as I was getting ready in my hotel room and just about to head down to the conference center and deliver my keynote address, I realized that I hadn't packed a dress shirt. My heart skipped a beat. But rather than panic, I decided to see the humor in it: I had a chuckle about how I might change the opening of my keynote to explain why I was wearing a T-shirt under my suit jacket. But then I noticed there was a mall not far from the conference center, and I had about fifteen minutes to spare. So, with my suit jacket flapping in the wind and my laptop bag under my arm, I jogged to the mall, bought the first shirt I found, and jogged back on time. Seeing the humor in the setback helped me get things back on track—and to my knowledge, nobody noticed that my sleeves were way too short or saw the gaudy flower buttons.

This particular strategy should be use selectively—it is not particularly appropriate for a major tragedy. But I have found it to be helpful when I have been faced with moderate challenges where I'm prone to exaggerating the impact. I've found when I've tried to view setbacks and mistakes through a humorous lens it helps prevent me from going into panic mode, where my problem-solving abilities are greatly reduced, and thus I'm able to evaluate my options with more clarity and find a way forward.

Put Setbacks into Perspective

Putting setbacks into perspective is another strategy I have used when I am tempted to give up rather than pull myself back on track. In the dress-shirt example, I might remind myself that this challenge is truly trivial—and one that is easy to solve compared to, say, a speaker in a wheelchair who is faced with an auditorium accessible only via stairs. Even many of the more distressing setbacks that I have experienced I have been able to work through by reminding myself how much more difficult many people have it than I do.

I cautioned in the Summit of Self-Respect about comparing yourselves to others who have it better than you, which makes it easy to feel like a victim; but when a comparison can help you—when it reminds you that you are *not* a victim—it's quite justified. In other words, look at the outcome. Ask yourself, is this comparison helpful in moving me forward?

Not only does putting setbacks into perspective help reduce panic and stress, it also seems to help generate a certain amount of inspiration to get things together and continue along the path you know you should follow. I have also realized the benefit of putting setbacks into perspective from comments and emails I have received from people who have attended one of my Everest presentations: often some version of, "If you guys can get through that, I can certainly get through this"—and then they share whatever that setback is.

You can also add perspective after the fact when you look back on a setback. This is what I sometimes refer to as the "It wasn't that bad" strategy. Often when we experience adversity or disaster, we replay the most cataclysmic version of the event when we remember and ruminate on it. By reminding ourselves that the outcome really wasn't that bad—we survived it, after all—we are able to better find ways of picking ourselves back up and getting back on track.

I have had to use this technique after calls with clients that seem to have gone awry or after I have put my foot in my mouth during a presentation or workshop. I came to realize how pointless and counterproductive it is to endlessly contemplate how bad things went. My goal is to learn from what happened rather than be consumed by it. And we often tend to remember situations as being much worse than they actually were, so we might as well soften the narrative. Even if what happened really is disastrous, there is no benefit in endlessly torturing yourself over it. Don't slide back down the ice face; just clean your ascender and keep going.

Set Time Limits

Another effective strategy to aid in increasing your resilience is to set time limits for yourself. This strategy works in the same way that the giant timer displayed at the finish line of a marathon race stimulates bone-weary runners to put that last bit of juice in to beat their target time. Bodybuilders, elite athletes, and military training regimes often use similar timed strategies in helping to build resilience. By setting yourself time limits, it creates a sense of urgency that can help inspire you to get back on your feet, literally or figuratively, before it is too late. Time limits seem to help curb our tendency to give up by tapping into the "now or never" thought patterns that stem from our concern about missing opportunities.

I am a strong advocate of this strategy and employ it frequently to boost my own resilience. I often set myself time limits when it comes to even small activities, as I am prone to allowing distractions to throw me off course. I have also used it many times in my hiking, biking, and mountaineering adventures. At times in the high altitude when I have been completely spent, I have often chosen a piece of ice or rock that I could see an ambitious distance ahead of me where I would allow myself to rest. I refer to this strategy as "choosing your own summit," and it is very powerful. When I finally do reach that point, I allow myself to rest only for a short time, which I track on my watch, before I force myself to get on my feet and choose another "summit" on the landscape ahead of me.

Look for Opportunities within Crisis

When everything seems to be falling apart and nothing turning in your favor, it is hard to see the opportunities that such chaos creates, but they are there if you take the time to flush them out. This is easier to say than to do, but it does work if you are willing to do the searching. It should be part of a broader mentality shift towards more positive and solution-focused thinking, but it is worth touching on again in the context of resilience.

In my own life, the COVID-19 pandemic was a good example of this. Around the beginning of 2020, all of the speaking engagements and training programs that I had in my calendar for the year came screeching to a halt and the cancellations flowed in, one wave after another. Naturally, this was a disastrous blow to my business and earning ability for the year, but after the initial shell shock I decided to look for opportunities rather than letting it hinder me.

It turned out that when I did start looking, I found many opportunities that helped to ameliorate the crisis my business was in and get me back on my feet. This book is one example of a project that would likely not have come together had I not had the additional time to focus. I also found opportunities for delivering virtual programs, which really took off in some sectors. Even the opportunity to spend more time with my kids at such a crucial time in their development was a blessing in disguise that I really appreciated.

Looking for opportunities in crisis will help you maneuver your way back on track sooner and more effectively. There is no point in brooding endlessly over what you cannot change. Focus on identifying the opportunities that will help you through tough situations and concentrate on those. If one route towards the peak is impassible, look for another.

Establish Support Systems

Resilience research consistently identifies social support as a major factor when it comes to individual resilience. This is one of the advantages of having a stable and supportive family, community, and resource network, which—as we have already seen—is a protective factor in the natural development of resilience. But even if you don't have that kind of structure, there are steps you can take to help establish your own social support so that you have people to lean on who can help you get back on your feet.

The first step is to take inventory of the friends and coworkers you spend the most time with and tend to hang out with. Especially in the era of social media, it is quite common to have many "friends" but to actually have zero or very few close friends that you can rely on. It turns out that quality is much more important than quantity when it comes to the social impact on resilience.

Sometimes it takes a crisis for people to realize that the friends they thought they had are more like acquaintances who make themselves scarce when really needed; but with a bit of foresight and effort, true friends can be identified even in the absence of crisis. If you do discover that most of your friendships are shallow, it is probably wise to spend less time with those people and focus on discovering and investing in deeper friendships with the people who will be there for you when you need them—and whom you trust and care about enough to be there for them no matter what as well. Such relationships need to be reciprocal, so you need to be honest with yourself and with your friends. If you want to be able to lean on someone, they need to be able to lean on you.

Healthy social relationships also help to lessen our stress response when faced with adversity, which is one of the reasons why it is important and beneficial to get involved in community groups, spiritual groups, philanthropy, professional associations, special interest groups, and other social groups where you have people around you that can provide some emotional support, a helping hand, a listening ear, or an audience to bounce ideas off of to help get you back on the right path.

Make the Commitment

In the end, it is up to you to make the commitment to becoming more resilient and, in turn, learning the skills and strategies that will aid you in this pursuit. It is a mentality and habitual shift more than a spur-of-the-moment decision if you are really going to bring about meaningful change in your level of resilience. If such a shift is important and meaningful to you, be mindful of your thoughts and actions when it comes to responding to adversity and focus on consciously and consistently bouncing back, even when the setbacks are minimal. If you want to be more resilient, these strategies are the route to the summit; it's up to you to take the steps.

Expedition Debrief

Do you consider yourself resilient, or could you be better at bouncing back? If you are like most of us, this is an area where you can see the benefits but might struggle to make progress. Your capacity to recover quickly when you are knocked down or thrown off of your path is just as important as your ability to start down such a path in the first place.

What can you do to strengthen your resilience? As we have seen, the route to resilience has countless small trials and tribulations along the way. Many of these setbacks seem inconsequential, but how you respond to the small obstacles ends up making all the difference. The unpredictable and volatile nature of your life and surroundings provides the perfect field for either strengthening or weakening your resilience, one small decision and one small action at a time.

It is worth understanding the risk factors and protective factors associated with resilience, since you have influence over some of them or can at least be aware of them for context and future planning. But you need to be careful not to let them define your future. Remember that there are many outliers in the data, people who can remain tremendously resilient despite having the odds stacked against them. This is where your focus should be: always building yourself up from your current state, like you would if you were strengthening a muscle. Even if you are weak, you can build resilience capacity through careful and consistent implementation.

In addition to tapping into your motivation strategies, which of the strategies we explored in this chapter are you willing to exercise? Through changing the way you view setbacks and incorporating some of the practical strategies we have covered, you can become a more resilient person. If you need some inspiration along the way, I have found it helpful to read about and connect with individuals who have transformed their lives in this regard—from helpless sufferers to confident trailblazers. Surround yourself with a network of people who will encourage and empower you to become more resilient. The ability to effect change is within your grasp if you can commit and make it a priority for your life.

SUMMIT SEVEN

THE SUMMIT OF SELF-ACTUALIZATION

My First Book

When I was in my youth, I don't remember ever planning or even wanting to write a book. But after my family's Everest expedition in 2008, I started doing more and more public speaking, and people would often come up afterwards and tell me, "You've got to write a book!" The first few times this happened I brushed off the idea, but gradually I started thinking more about whether I would have the discipline and ability to do it. And then I decided to try.

It took me about four years to write it. Too often, I found it difficult to muster the discipline to sit down and write. But I was fortunate to have kept a journal throughout the expedition, as many of my memories were fuzzy—a phenomenon that seems to be common among mountaineers due to the lack of oxygen.

When I thought I had finally finished writing, I started looking at publishing options. Self-publishing seemed the simplest route, but I realized it would limit my reach, and I was concerned about the lack of credibility in self-publishing—anybody can publish anything nowadays. Traditional publishers have standards and, more importantly in my mind, they have distribution channels and publishing relationships that allow for much greater reach. So I decided to contact as many publishers as possible. I set to work finding contact information, calling, emailing, and reaching out every way I could.

I soon found out that the publishing industry isn't the easiest to navigate. The vast majority of those I reached out to, left messages for, and emailed never got back to me even after multiple attempts. Those that did get back replied that they were not interested in working with first-time authors or that they only dealt with literary agents.

So, after my first round of disappointments, I decided to contact as many literary agents as I could. Unfortunately, all I got from those efforts were replies in a similar vein, asking for lengthy proposals or straight-up saying that they were not interested. I sent proposals to those who asked, but I never heard back. Overall, the industry seemed impenetrable for a first-time author. After six or eight months of this, I was starting to lose hope and beginning to think that if I wanted my book to be published, I would have to self-publish after all.

While I was pondering my options and hashing out a plan for what to do next, a colleague recommended that I reach out to a small publisher in Renfrew, Ontario, called General Store Publishing House (GSPH). I called them up right away and found myself talking to the founder and manager. The conversation wasn't too different from those I'd had with other publishers— general disinterest. However, he did give me the option that if I paid one of his editors $200 to read through my manuscript, the editor would write a short evaluation, which they would review in-house to gauge interest.

After hanging up the telephone, I remember thinking to myself, "What a money grab that is! Might as well flush it down the toilet!"

After thinking it over awhile, however, I decided that since I didn't really have many other options, perhaps I should just pay and see what happened. After all, I would also receive a copy of the evaluation, which might shed some light on my writing. I went ahead and sent a check to the editor along with a printout of my manuscript.

To my surprise, I got a call from the publisher two weeks later. That second call had a whole different tone, as he explained that he wasn't sure what I had put into my book, but his editor thought it was terrific! He had written a glowing review, and GSPH was interested. Naturally I was thrilled with the conclusion as well—I finally had a prospective publisher and things were moving forward!

I was first offered a traditional publishing contract, which has the advantage of the publisher covering all the production costs and thus taking all the risk. With traditional contracts, the house and any affiliates, such as distributors and bookstores, control all aspects of publishing. If only a few hundred copies of the book ever sell, the publishing house loses a significant amount of money in the end, which is why they are understandably cautious and selective on which books they publish. And since they've taken the majority of the risk, they also take the majority of any profits; for each book that sells for $25 in a bookstore, the author generally only receives $1 to $2.

I was also offered a copublishing agreement, however, in which we would split the up-front costs, thus sharing the risk, and we would have a more equal share in revenues, should there be any going forward. I decided that if I was going to be fully committed to personally putting my time and energy into trying to make the book a success, then I had better take the copublishing option where I had more skin in the game, so to speak.

But the process wasn't nearly over yet. I had thought my part was more or less done—I had spent years writing the book, and now it was finished—but that wasn't exactly true. It still needed editing. I got aligned with an editor, and we went back and forth, adding sections, modifying sections, and removing significant portions. I ended up working through the book from cover to cover numerous times.

Finally, we went to print and the first ten boxes of books arrived at our home. I had published my first book, *The Family that Conquered Everest*, in June of 2014, and I was thrilled about it. What a satisfying feeling it was to finally have a physical book in my hands after so many years.

Because of the up-front financial investment, I had to personally sell around 1,500 copies before breaking even, so I set to work trying to make it happen. I organized a launch at a local event center to raise awareness, I started doing frequent signings at bookstores around the area, and I tried to do as much speaking as I could, making signed copies available afterwards for those who wanted one. After a full year of promoting and selling, I finally managed to reach my goal. I had been ordering more copies fairly steadily from GSPH, and they were pretty well out of stock at their warehouse from the initial print run. I emailed to discuss a possible reprint as I was running low again.

That is when I received a phone call from the publisher. The publishing house had been purchased by various entities and printing companies over the years, and the company that made the latest acquisition had decided to shut down GSPH. It is difficult for smaller houses to try to compete with the large entities and online platforms, so they decided to pull the plug. The publisher was deeply sorry about everything but explained that there wasn't anything he could do about it at that point. I don't fault him or his staff, as they all seemed as surprised and disappointed as I was. We parted on good terms, I was able to purchase the few remaining books they still had in stock, and that was that.

My heart was pretty heavy about the way everything unfolded. What a disaster, I thought! I had just spent countless hours and a huge amount of my energy and attention for an entire year, not to mention the effort in the preceding years, and, in the end, it was mostly all in vain, as I would have to fall back on my last-resort option of self-publishing. I could not imagine a more ill-fated ending to my publishing journey.

I had learned the lesson of perseverance: in spite of all the odds and opposition, I had gotten my book published. But there was another lesson I had yet to learn: the lesson of perspective. As most of us would, I saw the situation only through the lens of the moment. And through that lens, it looked like a disaster. But, as has happened so many times to so many people, that "disaster" turned out to be the door to opportunity.

An author who signs a publishing agreement with a publisher has to sign over almost all of the book rights, since publishers usually take a significant risk when committing to publishing a book. This was the case for me. But there is always a clause in a publishing agreement about what happens to the rights if the publishing house is dissolved or enters a state of insolvency. Most commonly, the rights revert back to the author. And this was the case for me.

At first I thought, "Yes, but who cares? I've already been through the rejection process with the larger publishers, and now I'm back where I started." There was some truth in this, but the situation, and thus the resulting conversations with publishers, was different the second time around. I already had a published book at that point. Not only that, I had sold 1,500 copies in a relatively short time. It was also clear from the feedback and reviews that people liked my book, and I had started to build a following. The result was that I was able to talk to, and eventually sign on with, a much larger publisher, that had more extensive distribution networks and relationships. We also revamped the book, giving it a new cover, going through another round of edits, and including full-color images throughout. I'm amazed at how many places the book is available around North America and beyond, and in various formats. My wife, kids, and I did a mini-vacation to California a few years back, and I ended up doing a number of signings at bookstores along the coast, two thousand miles away from where we live.

Getting Your Life in Order

Some of you may have read this far in this book and still be thinking, "That's easy for you to say, you don't have my challenges."
But my point is, however far down the mountain you are, you
can always climb. Start where you are, with all your shortcomings, disadvantages, pathologies, failings, inequities, and other
challenges, and work at making one thing better in your life each
day. This is the path forward.

Remember Maslow's hierarchy, from the Summit of Self-
Motivation? The top of it is self-actualization. This is what we
are building towards. But we need to have the lower levels in
order first. Just as a person who is starving for food doesn't give
much thought to preserving the environment and a person who
is fleeing persecution doesn't prioritize intimacy, if we haven't
satisfied our basic human needs, we aren't at a point where
we are able to focus on self-actualization. This may sound self-
evident, but I know many people—and continue to meet people
on a regular basis—whose lives are a complete disaster in terms
of their health, family, finances, and mental state, yet they are
convinced that what they need to focus on is a creative project
they've been inspired to pursue on a whim. Don't fall for the
illusion that if only you write a book, get a promotion, win a car,
or secure an important contract, then your life will be turned
around. It just doesn't work like that.

This is in part where I think some of the negativity towards
self-help stems from. Just as some people view any kind of
weight-loss program as a fad diet, there are people who will label
any kind of positive or life-enriching material as emotional snake
oil. Some of them talk about their lives and how positive thinking
and self-help gurus have made them that much worse. When I
read this, it makes me think about how much they could benefit from practicing that which they heatedly condemn, if only
they would make a true commitment. Consciously or subconsciously, they've fallen victim to their own prejudices; they've

superficially tried a few techniques so that they can write them off and further justify their own misery.

In truth, there was a time when I was very much like that. I didn't believe any mind games or mental exercises could really make a difference in my life. But eventually I reached a point where I decided to really give some of the ideas and techniques I had been reading about a proper and committed test in my own life. It took a while before I was able to see significant benefit, but it did make a difference. And it makes perfect sense why the changes took time. It takes us years and years to develop detrimental beliefs and thinking patterns. When it takes that long to learn a habit, it is going to take a lot of time to unlearn it or replace it with a superior habit.

This is the point I want to start this chapter with: Meaning, contentment, and self-fulfillment come from building a foundation of success, starting with working on the foundational aspects of your life. Pursing a fad or a lofty whim in the realm of self-actualization when your foundational needs are faltering is a recipe for a short-term shot in the dark followed by relapse and giving up. In other words, don't choose Everest or K2 as your first mountain to climb without any preparation or training. You are setting yourself up for disaster if you neglect building the technical and physical foundation on lesser magnitude mountains first. The same applies to self-actualization and what I would consider the related higher-order aspects of personal growth and fulfillment.

That doesn't mean don't set ambitious self-actualization goals for yourself. I'm a big believer in setting ambitious goals in all areas of our lives, whether they seem obtainable in our current state or not. What I am saying relates back to what we have seen on the previous summits: you need to know yourself and really understand what you need and want before you can decide where to focus your energy. Building a house that will survive the storms starts with pouring a solid foundation, and the keystone cannot be supported until all the other stones are in place. You can't climb from Camp 3 when you're still on the trail to Base Camp.

Proactive versus Reactive Living

There are two modes of approaching the influence we have on our lives: proactive living and reactive living. The majority of people I know or encounter in my daily interactions live in reactive mode.

What I mean by reactive living is that those who are in this mode behave as though life simply happens to them. They react to what the world throws at them each day, and their emotions and behaviors predictably reflect their external circumstances with little or no conscious interjection. This is an accidental way of living: like leaves in the autumn breeze, waiting to find out which way the wind will blow us and where we will end up. It is the default mode, requiring little thought and energy.

It should be no surprise that when we are in reactive mode, since there is little incentive to plan for the future or delay gratification, we are more prone to pursuing expedient pleasures and satisfying our immediate emotional needs with external stimuli, since we never know whether luck will bring them to us again. Likewise with the negatives: we wait until we get a wet foot and then we get out the rubber boots; we wait until our house gets broken into and then we get an alarm system; we wait until the boss retires before we try to move up the corporate hierarchy; we wait until the avalanche comes before we move the tent. Reactive living takes minimal up-front effort, which is why it is so tempting, but it is unsatisfying and unfulfilling in the end.

A variation of reactive living is kind of a hybrid, where a person is perpetually waiting for the opportune time to take action. They have a proactive plan, but they just never get to it. The timing is never right, and "someday" soon becomes "never."

Proactive living is a whole different mindset; it is a mindset of internal control and life on purpose. When living in proactive mode, we live life intentionally, empowered with the conviction that we can set our own sails and end up wherever we want. People living proactively use their time, energy, creativity, and skills to pursue their passions and solve problems that they have strategically identified with intention. Their motives are clear, and they have a plan of attack so that life become far less sporadic. Balancing risk and developing support structures keeps life fun and interesting.

If you are living reactively, it is time to take back the reins. Create a game plan that involves clear goals and dreams that you have identified. Then be mindful of your actions so that you aren't always putting out fires. Instead, you are intentionally navigating the landscape and choosing which interesting challenges you want to tackle. Proactive living is a much more meaningful and fulfilling way to move through life.

Going Beyond the Comfort Zone

A week after our honeymoon, Natalie and I made a commitment to step a bit further out of our comfort zones: we packed our bags and moved to Santiago, Chile.

I recommend that newlyweds take part in a life-changing experience like this or something similar. It enables a deeper bonding and strengthening of interdependence because spouses have to rely on each other in working through challenges and disagreements rather than running to friends, parents, or other family members. Family members mean well, but their influences and opinions often give couples excuses for not tackling important relationship issues head-on.

Santiago was a whole new world for us. I knew a bit of Spanish from a course I had taken in university, but I wasn't prepared for complete immersion. The first engineering project that I was assigned to when I arrived in Chile was a project for a local mining company. Since our client did not want any English reports for that particular project, the vast majority of the employees hired for the project communicated only in Spanish. It was challenging enough trying to navigate the city with my "tourist" level of Spanish, but to be conversing in technical engineering terms and reviewing Spanish documents was a stretch, to say the least.

There were a handful of other expatriates from English-speaking countries in the Chilean office. The temptation was to gravitate to that which was known and comfortable. The expatriates would frequently organize their own social events and would most often stick together at work as well. Many of the expatriates who had been there for years could still hardly order a beer in Spanish and knew next to nothing of the culture. They had fashioned a pleasant and comfortable subculture of their own with their circles of expatriate friends and coworkers.

Natalie and I decided that we weren't going to follow that same path. We didn't spend a lot of time at expatriate social gatherings. We instead decided to make efforts to get to know Chileans and try to make some Chilean friends.

I was seated in the office at a cubicle next to a young man name Giancarlo, who was a native Chilean. He knew only a few words in English, so we communicated almost exclusively through my broken Spanish. I kept a translation program open on my computer so I could quickly look up words. After a few weeks, Giancarlo and I started to form a friendship, and he invited me and Natalie over for dinner to meet his wife, Pili. Our first get-together was rather awkward, since we could only bumble through fairly shallow conversations with our limited vocabulary, but the next week we had them over to our apartment for dinner, and then we kept alternating these get-togethers each week. Natalie and I were exhausted at the end of each day, trying to sort out all the Spanish, but we learned quickly. After about a month, we decided to take a three-day vacation with Giancarlo and Pili, flying down to the lakes region of Chile, where we did some white-water rafting and hiking. It ended up being one of many adventures we shared with them over the nearly two years we lived in Chile.

Within a month of arriving in Chile, we had also joined a local club that organized day hikes in the Andes mountains and foothills. After our first hike, everyone got together for a barbecue at the trailhead, where there was a small park. I was telling a story in my broken Spanish as we ate, and I had meant to use the phrase "¡Qué pena!"—which means "What a pity!"—but I accidentally said "¡Qué pene!"—which means "What a penis!" A number of the guys around the table jumped up, smiling, and exclaimed "¡Gracias!" jokingly thanking me for the compliment. We all had a good laugh, and situations like that were how I learned the language, one awkward mistake at a time. I learned to speak Spanish quite well in the time we lived in Chile and eventually got to the point where I was delivering my Everest presentation entirely in Spanish for various groups.

There are dangerous areas throughout Chile, so we had to do our research and be aware, but we didn't let fear prevent us from experiencing all that the beautiful country had to offer. Almost every weekend we were on a new adventure, from exploring the Atacama Desert in the north and surfing waves in secluded coastal villages to hiking circuits in the Patagonia region and visiting the mo'ai stone heads on Easter Island. It was a truly remarkable and life-enriching experience all around for us.

I was also still working through my mental health challenges in those years, and I had decided to push myself into new situations whenever I could, even if they were uncomfortable, so that I could continue to grow. It was a form of exposure therapy, and helped me to learn and mature rapidly. I had made the decision to not let anxiety or social embarrassment cripple me anymore and I stuck to it.

The Growth Zone

Unless we deliberately make choices that push us beyond our comfort zones, we end up corralled inside them. This is where the vast majority of people spend most of their lives. It feels safe and secure operating within the environments that are known, so it is perceived as much less stressful—and often it *is* much less stressful. Within our comfort zone there is generally a lot less risk, and we feel in control.

At the edge of our comfort zone is our *fear barrier*, which keeps most people from pushing farther. It isn't hard to come up with reasons not to cross the fear barrier; there are plenty of excuses and procrastination techniques. But the problem with living within the comfort zone is that complacency and stagnation set in. I would argue that it is impossible to fulfill our potential and live in meaningful ways without stepping outside of the known.

On the other hand, there is also a segment of the population that lives and operates in what we could refer to as the *danger zone*. This is the chaotic region on the far side of the fear barrier, where individuals throw logic and planning to the wind. Those operating in the danger zone live only for the moment and lust for excitement, pleasure, reckless decisions, and frivolous actions. The danger zone is thrilling, but spending too much time in it is a recipe for real psychological, financial, and even physical harm.

But there is also a narrow band that straddles the fear barrier and is partially in both the comfort zone and the danger zone. This is the area that we can call the *growth zone*, where we have roots within our comfort zone but are continuously breaking through the fear barrier to explore the beginnings of the danger zone. We have to take risks to live in the growth zone, but we mitigate the risks through our connection with the known and the stability that it provides for exploration. We maintain a degree of security and control over our lives while continuously discovering new ideas and working through new challenges. This is the zone where self-actualization occurs.

LIVING WITHIN YOUR GROWTH ZONE

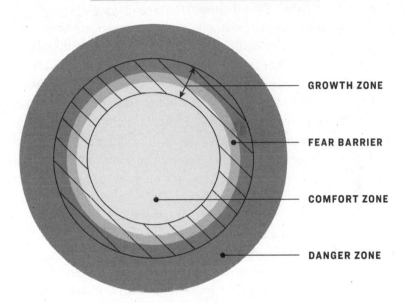

GROWTH ZONE

FEAR BARRIER

COMFORT ZONE

DANGER ZONE

As your comfort zone expands, you remain in your growth zone by continuing to push beyond your new fear barrier.

We usually think of "playing it safe" as the securest way to go through life, but this isn't always the case. As time progresses, what we cling to as safe and secure doesn't always remain safe and secure. Change is inevitable, and we can never be certain that following and maintaining the status quo will shield us. By definition, taking risks involves exposing ourselves to uncertainty as well as to the possibility of undesirable outcomes. This is usually emotionally unsettling; although some people are more affected than others, humans are inherently risk-averse, meaning that we feel losses more strongly than gains. From a personality perspective, the propensity to take risks is correlated with both openness and extraversion. It is also negatively correlated with conscientiousness and agreeableness, meaning individuals high in conscientiousness and agreeableness are less likely to take risks.

It turns out that the more calculated risks we take, the better we become at choosing paths that minimize the likelihood of negative outcomes and maximize the likelihood of positive outcomes. This is why it is important to take small risks early in life, so that if we fail, it is a learning experience rather than a complete catastrophe. When individuals have seldom had to weigh risks throughout their lives and are suddenly put into roles or situations where they have to make decisions based on relative risk, they are far more likely to fail. Keep this in mind when it comes to your own risk-taking appetite. It is OK to be relatively risk-averse, but you need to take some risks in life if you want to gain new knowledge and perspectives. You want to put yourself in situations where you can fail on smaller scales and learn so you can avoid catastrophic failures later on.

Risk avoidance often extends to the workplace. Since employees are poorly equipped to assess and weigh risk themselves, the trend has been towards ensuring every activity has an established step-by-step procedure for workers to follow. In this way, there is no need for workers to use their own abilities to assess and respond to risk. It isn't as though procedures don't have a place; I worked in the nuclear industry for a few years, and almost everything was procedure driven because of the high consequences of mistakes. Procedures also allow us to ensure consistency and bring together best practices, rather than reinventing the wheel each time we go through an activity. But we need to guard against reducing workers to compliant robots following the pre-established steps rather than recognizing them as intellectual individuals who can think critically about alternatives and innovate to find better ways.

Innovation is more and more important in today's fast-paced and ever-changing world. We need to adapt to changes and figure out more effective ways of solving problems or we will be left behind. And as technology continues to advance, procedural-type jobs are disappearing at an alarming rate. If a job calls for a compliant robot, a compliant robot can be built and run for less money than a messy human. Since step-by-step operations can most easily be automated, the need for assembly line workers, mail sorters, switchboard operators, typists, and countless similar tradespeople is dwindling towards zero. These are frightening trends, especially for people reliant on such jobs for their livelihoods. But the important thing to take away from this trend is that it is our ability to think critically and creatively that will be of most value in future, rather than our ability to follow pre-established steps.

And that is why I believe that taking calculated risks is so important throughout life. We will make mistakes along the way, this is inevitable, but the knowledge and habits of thought we gain from such mistakes are essential parts of our development. As the founder of Facebook, Mark Zuckerberg, put it, "The biggest risk is not taking any risk. In a world that's changing really quickly, the only strategy that is guaranteed to fail is not taking risks."

Self-Advocacy

The concept of self-advocacy is one I touched on at the beginning of this book, but in many respects, a lot of the other areas we have covered, such as self-knowledge, self-respect, self-worth, and self-motivation, are prerequisites for self-advocacy, or at least are highly interdependent.

Jim Rohn has a quote I like that relates to self-advocacy: "If you don't design your own life plan, chances are you'll fall into someone else's plan. And guess what they have planned for you? Not much." That's bit blunt, but it's true: if we wait around for others to advocate for us, chances are we will be waiting a very long time. True, we have family members, friends, colleagues, and others who advocate for us at various times throughout our lives, but it's intermittent and can't always be counted on—and in some cases, there is an unwritten expectation of reciprocation or indebtedness.

And yet many of us are socialized to believe that self-advocacy is wrong or even immoral: it is selfish to focus on our own aspirations when we should be putting the needs of others first. But while social concern that results in actions carried out for the good of others is a cornerstone of proper socialization, we can become doormats if we allow others to constantly step on us, silence us, and take advantage of us—and inside we will be frustrated and resentful.

On the other end of the spectrum, however, we can be so focused on advocating for ourselves that we end up becoming aggressive bullies. In an effort to make sure our own needs and aspirations are met, we neglect the needs of others, which results in the development of anger and resentment in those around us. Obviously, as with many of the other concepts we've explored, there is a balance that needs to be maintained. But we need to be ready, willing, and able to advocate for ourselves.

One of the areas where I discovered the importance of advocating for myself was when it came to my grades in school. I found out fairly early on that although some teachers truly had an interest in the lives and success of their students, there were also many who mainly wanted to make their job as simple as possible while still doing enough to get paid. In subjects such as math and some science classes, I didn't have many concerns, because the answers were either right or wrong, and if I got it wrong, it was my own error, and I would work to improve for next time. But in courses like history and English, essays were commonly assigned, and work was assessed through more subjective methods. Some of my teachers were fond of assigning nearly all the students a mark somewhere between 75 and 85 percent for essays, since it was a convenient way to stay in alignment with expected averages without having to mark on a curve. My problem was that I was hoping to apply to universities where the acceptance criteria required averages in the high eighties. One particularly stubborn teacher insisted to me that she just didn't give out marks in the nineties when marking essays, no matter how good the content was. I decided to push back and contest any marks that I didn't think accurately assessed the work. Naturally, not all of my teachers appreciated this (though some were happy that I was taking their course seriously). I maintained this approach throughout university, often meeting with my professors after class if I thought something seemed amiss with a mark. I found that marking mistakes were fairly common because my profes- sors were either exhausted or they had their teaching assistants marking papers to save them the effort. Having taught a few years as a college professor, I can relate to the exhaustion after marking hundreds of exams late into the night.

When I started my engineering career, I soon found out that if I was going to get involved in interesting projects and advance in the company, I couldn't simply wait around, year after year, in the hopes that my managers would advocate for me. I had some good managers and some terrible managers, but, in general, they were primarily concerned about their own career progression and how managing their subordinates best fit into that agenda. That's how it goes: they had to advocate for themselves as well. I was falling into their plans, and they didn't have much planned for me. I did get the opportunity to work on some really inter- esting projects in some really interesting areas with some really interesting people—but none of that happened by chance or by waiting for the tides to turn in my favor. In each instance, I advocated for the opportunities, usually going well above my managers so that I could build relationships with those in the company who had the authority to make it happen.

There was a limit to such advancement, though, and it seemed to be primarily dictated by the number of years employ- ees had worked for the firm, rather than by actual performance or project outcomes. This didn't seem to provide any tangible achievement I could work towards, other than growing old. I felt like I was no longer personally growing. In one of my last annual career development meetings, I asked my manager what I could do to continue advancing within the company, and he said, "You have to put in your time." I thought a lot about that and finally decided it was time for me to move on.

I remember being mildly annoyed when I was young every time a parent or educator would repeat the cliché, "If you love what you do for work, you'll never have to work a day in your life!" I used to think, "What a pile of crap that is! We call it *work* for a reason: it is supposed to be miserable. Otherwise we'd call it *play* or *fun!*" Perhaps this was because, when I was growing up, I didn't really know anyone who actually liked their work. I knew plenty of people who begrudgingly dragged themselves to the office, and many others who whined and complained about their jobs, so I thought that was how it was. But I've changed my tune on this. The average person spends more than ninety thousand hours of their lives working, or about a third of our waking hours here on Earth. It is worth thinking long and hard about the degree to which the work you are engaged in is fulfilling and brings meaning to your life. The advice I would give is to not let other people have too much influence on what you decide to do for a living, including any career changes.

When I decided to leave my engineering position to pursue a career in speaking and training, I had countless people try vigorously to talk me out of it. Many of these people were friends, family, and others who were very close to me, people I know and trust, and that weighed heavily on my mind. I was told a number of times that I would be a fool to leave a pensioned engineering position to pursue such a frivolous ambition. But in the end, I did it anyways. I wasn't positive it was the right move to make, but I didn't want to always be looking back and wondering what it would have been like had I had the courage to try it. I was motivated by a mix of curiosity, challenge, personal growth, and the freedom to carve my own path through life.

If you're thinking about committing to a courageous and atypical ambition in your life, you'll have the same types of naysayers and critics. If it is something you are really passionate about, my advice would be to ignore the naysayers and follow your own path. If it is music, pursue that. If it is art, pursue that. If it is business, pursue that. Be smart about it, do your research, and have a plan—but don't put it off for any longer than absolutely necessary. Life is short and you never know what day will be your last.

I can honestly say that I have found a vocation that I truly love. If you're still a skeptic about whether work could ever actually be enjoyable, I'm here to tell you that it can. It isn't as though it doesn't have its challenges, but I am excited for each new challenge, each new place I get to visit, and each new group of individuals I have the privilege of working with. It is truly fulfilling and enriching work that keeps me excited, continues to push me beyond my comfort zone, and gives me the satisfaction that I'm making a difference.

Purposeful Living

When we explored concepts like motivation and discipline throughout this book, these could be considered the what and the how in our lives, but there is a deeper influence that we've touched on a few times that warrants further exploration. This underlying influence is what we call *purpose*, which we could rightly consider our *why*.

There is a quote I like from the Austrian psychiatrist Viktor Frankl, a Holocaust survivor who was imprisoned in Auschwitz and other Nazi concentration camps from 1942 to 1945. Frankl wrote in his 1946 book *Man's Search for Meaning* that "He who has a why to live for can bear with almost any how," paraphrasing Friedrich Nietzsche's writing from 1889. This quote captures why purpose is so important as well as how purpose affords us the motivation and energy to fulfill our destiny.

In many ways, purposeful living is the ultimate summit that we are shooting for, the apex in our lives that guides all of the goals, decisions, and actions we embrace along the way. Living purposefully can also be referred to as intentional living; since our journey is aligned with a deliberate and overarching ambition, our actions are less random. This leads to more stability and a sense of meaning arising from the perception that what we are doing matters. Our purpose guides us in how we make decisions, plan our future, choose goals, seek out friends, resolve conflicts, and make sense of suffering and hardships throughout life.

People often say that they have "discovered" their true purpose in life. This is an insightful way of referring to it because, as much as there is an aspect of choice, purpose does seem to be something that we identify based on what feels right and what brings us fulfillment. In this sense, discovering our purpose is exactly why deep introspection and exploration of our personality traits as well as our motivations is so critical. It is through this that we truly discover our purpose, and it isn't so much a rigid realization as it is a fluid process—we often evolve our purpose based on our priorities, experiences, and interactions throughout life.

Some people's purposes are relatively shallow. It seems that when we have done very little introspection and are living primarily in reactive mode, life tends to create a superficial purpose for us that is related to survival. This purpose is accompanied by a series of desires that are more or less aligned with our basic needs and biological impulses. We could say that our overall purpose in this case becomes to survive through attaining food, clothing, and shelter while at the same time deriving pleasure through expedient and convenient means. It is hard to say whether this should really be considered a purpose in life, since it is mostly biological, but it does keep people moving forward. Without any purpose at all, people would—and some do—simply waste away to their own demise.

Another important point is that, although we generally refer to purpose in the positive sense, not every purpose is positive or beneficial. Revenge, for example, can become a purpose for some; even destruction and obliteration can be a purpose for those who succumb to nihilism. The psychological way that such purposes streamline individual choices and actions throughout life can be just as potent as positive purposes, but their consequences can be terrible.

The point we are leading to—the summit—is the more profound and fulfilling purpose that brings positive meaning to our lives. This is the *higher purpose*: the summit that is above and beyond you, out in the real world. Your Summit of Self-Actualization, your higher purpose, comes through aligning personally meaningful accomplishments with activities that contribute to the greater good.

Focus

Understanding the principals of focus is an important and integral part of understanding and implementing a lot of the strategies we have covered throughout this book. It is also a key component of self-actualization.

The first thing to understand about focus is that people see things through different lenses. This can help bring together diverse thoughts and perspectives. Lenses are not all equally well-defined or helpful; some are clouded and fuzzy and some appear to be blatantly obstructed. But there are many viable lenses, some quite different from one another.

The second, and more pertinent, thing to understand about focus is how it influences our emotions, behaviors, and actions. This is why we need to take a conscious and careful approach to what we focus on.

When Natalie and I lived in Arizona, we decided to purchase a relatively high-end digital single-lens reflex camera, and I set to work studying the fundamentals of photography. I found it quite intriguing how the various settings and adjustments all work in unison, affecting and relying on each other: focus, aperture, shutter speed, and ISO (sensitivity). And they can tell us something about the effects of mental focus.

Focus is obviously important so that subjects aren't blurry, but depth of field—that is to say, how far in front of and behind your exact point of focus the image still looks sharp—plays an important role: how much of the picture is in focus?

The aperture setting works in a similar way to how dilated your eye's pupil is in any given light, and it is what determines the depth of field. The more open the aperture is, the more light passes through the lens but the shallower the depth of field becomes.

This is where shutter speed is important, which is how long the sensor is exposed to the light. If the aperture is smaller, the shutter speed needs to be slower to allow in sufficient light, but this can make images blurry if the object or the camera is moving during the short time the shutter is open.

Lastly, the camera's ISO setting refers to the light sensitivity of the digital image sensor. A higher sensitivity allows for faster shutter speed or a smaller aperture, but images become grainy if the sensitivity is pushed too high.

It is a complex balance of all these factors that creates the technically perfect image.

Your own focus and attention are a bit like this. Your aperture setting is how narrowly you fixate on issues rather than allowing peripheral details to influence you. This affects your depth of field, as you can either mostly ignore or attend to the details of the background and foreground.

Your shutter speed is how long you concentrate on specific issues. Do you allow enough time for details to be processed? Are you concentrating to the point where rumination takes over? There is often an optimal amount of time for concentration, which is where techniques like the time blocking strategy I outlined in the Summit of Self-Balance are so important.

Lastly, your ISO setting is your sensitivity to the issues you are focusing on. Your individual personality plays a major role in predetermining your sensitivity to issues, but so do your sleep patterns and other physiological factors. More broadly, your sensitivity is also affected by your experiences, socialization, upbringing, and education, as this all influences your ability to empathize and understand what is being seen. Some of the mindfulness techniques we explored in the Summit of Self-Regulation allow you to lower your ISO settings and become more detached from ruminating thought patterns, for example.

There is a popular theory about focus that has been coined and marketed as the law of attraction. Its premise is that our dominant thoughts, if cultivated properly and believed in with conviction, attract things into our lives through energy vibrations throughout the universe that enable such thoughts to be manifested into reality. I agree that our focus and dominant thoughts are critical, but I don't think we need such a mystical explanation. Purposeful changes occur when we understand and apply the complex relationships between our focus, our thought patterns, our mental imagery and associations, our emotional responses, our motivations, our sensory awareness, our ability to capitalize, our commitments, our resulting actions, and ultimately the resilience and perseverance that sustain these actions through to fruition.

The key thing to realize is that it involves more than just thinking. It involves many of the concepts and strategies that we have been exploring throughout this book. But it starts with focus.

Making Your Mind Work for You

Let's use an example to look at how to put this all into practice. Say that you have been overweight most of your life and really want to lose body fat. Thinking your way to weight loss just isn't going to cut it. It is only through consistent action that this is going to happen. So how might this happen in the context of what we just explored?

Weight loss is a complex issue. We are dealing with a multifaceted blend of competing motivations and desires. Many of these are largely biological in origin and are synchronized unconsciously; some are more psychological. There are countless weight-loss programs out there, but the fundamental principle is that the human body is governed by energy balance: if we take in fewer calories than we burn, we will lose weight. But there are many ways to do this, and different things may work for different people. For limiting calorie intake, a plan can prescribe limiting quantities, or consuming specific foods and drinks that make us feel full sooner or are less likely to be stored as fat, or making behavioral and lifestyle changes to reduce the urge to consume calories. For increasing calorie expenditure, further lifestyle changes and exercise routines can be recommended. A weight-loss plan can also work on the psychological side to reduce our urges to consume excess calories and increase our urges to burn them, including giving motivation through means such as accountability and getting our money's worth (weight-loss programs are often expensive). For someone like me, competitiveness can be effective. Some years ago, my wife and I challenged each other to a weight-loss contest, and my focus and mental imagery were primarily pegged on the personal satisfaction of winning rather than on looking better or feeling healthier. I ended up losing fourteen pounds in a little less than a month (and, yes, that's probably a bit more than is usually recommended in that time), primarily through the mental strategies that we've been discussing throughout this book.

And that's where we're headed with this: finding your focus and motivation, and applying these techniques in a focused and integrated way. You might start with asking yourself, "Why do I want to lose weight?" This is where introspection and self-knowledge are important. If your motivation is a slight inconvenience or social pressure, you are unlikely to succeed. You are contending with tremendous biological and psychological forces, so it had better be deeply important and meaningful to you.

Once you have established a good why, and you understand the what—burn more calories than you consume—your next step will be the how. Here is an example of how you might use the principles of focus and thought progression for something like weight loss.

You start with your focus. Weight loss has to be something that you are concentrating on frequently, or you won't be compelled to act. This involves directing your attention and not being hijacked by distractions. Exercises like the deliberate contemplation in the Summit of Self-Regulation can help develop this ability.

Notice your thought patterns when you think about losing weight. Do you automatically see yourself as a failure? Do you think you deserve to have the body shape you desire? Thought patterns are like habits. If you've repeated the same course of thinking long enough, they become automatic. The same thing applies to your self-talk. Are you writing yourself off as a letdown before you even begin? Chances are, if you haven't been successful with weight loss in the past, you have some work to do in these areas. The exercise of identifying the positives in the Summit of Self-Regulation is helpful for influencing thought patterns. Focus on consciously changing your thought patterns and on the nature of your self-talk. Notice the images and mental movies you have about yourself in your mind; use the technique of rewriting the ending to see your body transformed into the shape you want. Build mental associations between the image of yourself as you want to be and other positive elements in your life, both current and projected.

This will affect the emotions you have in relation to the steps you need to take. You want to get to the point where you subconsciously have positive emotions associated with doing the right things and negative emotions associated with doing the wrong things. The stronger these emotions are, the better. As we have already explored in depth, your motivations are primarily a response to how you feel, especially if you are low in conscientiousness, so the emotional changes are critical.

This is where sensory awareness is important. We have already explored in the Summit of Self-Regulation how we can only consciously process a small fraction of the millions of signals we receive through our five senses. Once you are focused and motivated towards a certain goal, you start to notice more of the opportunities and encouragement that will help get you there rather than the potential roadblocks that will send you off course. At that point you have to be open to capitalizing on opportunities that present themselves—and avoiding things that will derail you. Because much of the progression from thinking to action happens subconsciously, you won't always understand why you are drawn towards certain decisions, but you should pay close attention to intuitions, since this is how your unconscious mind communicates with your conscious mind.

Obviously, you can just use your rational mind to force yourself to take action, but without the other important steps in your thought progression, you won't have the motivation to persevere for very long. A common result of this is what's often called yo-yo dieting.

The steps in the progression we just went through aren't always sequential. Sometimes multiple steps happen almost simultaneously, which is why the interconnections between the different steps are the important parts. The goal is motivated and committed action that doesn't require an exhausting and unsustainable level of willpower. This is the point you want to get to, a point that allows you to bring about lasting change.

Streamline Your Efforts

When it comes to the aspects of life that we do want to change, it is important to put them through a kind of litmus test first. I often share this as a schematic in my programs showing the intersection of three circles. In the first circle are things that matter, in the second circle are things that we can influence, and in the third circle are things that we are willing to influence.

If we listen to the idle chit-chat of people on the street, in the subway, or on their phones, most of the complaints people have are about things that don't fall into one or more of these circles. They complain about the weather, grumble about politics, get upset about the economy, resent their boss, and have countless other gripes but don't plan on actually doing anything about them. If the issue that we are upset with does not satisfy all three circles, we need to let it go. We are wasting our energy by focusing on it and complaining about it. We should simply accept the things we cannot change, or are unwilling to change, and move on.

The area where all three circles overlap is the area to focus your attention: things that matter to you, that you can influence, and that you are willing to influence. That is how you find your route to the summit. Now start taking steps.

WHAT TO CONCENTRATE YOUR ENERGY ON

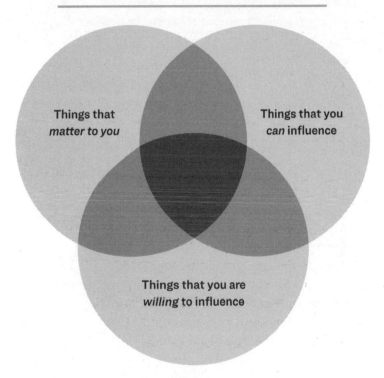

Things that *matter to you*

Things that you *can* influence

Things that you are *willing* to influence

Expedition Debrief

This final summit is in many ways the culmination of many of the other concepts we have explored on the previous summits. Self-actualization is the pinnacle of psychological development where you are able to cultivate and manifest your full potential.

How can you start to be more conscious about your focus and attention rather than allowing it to wander? It is usual to simply focus on whatever grabs your attention in the moment, but remember the basics of focus as you go about your daily routine. The valence of your thoughts matters, and you can consciously choose where you direct your attention.

What changes do you need to make to ensure you are living within the growth zone, where you are persistently breaking through your fear barrier to continuously improve? Remember that you don't want to leap chaotically into the danger zone, but you do need to take calculated risks and spend time outside of your comfort zone.

Are you living a purposeful and fulfilling life? Advocate for yourself so that you are living your life on purpose rather than completely dependent on the winds of fate to move you in whatever direction they happen to be blowing. Dig deep in determining your purpose, either through discovery or decision, and align your efforts and energy so that you are constantly moving towards a place that you find valuable and that matters to you.

Remember Maslow's pyramid. There is a reason why it also resembles the shape of a mountain. Start at the bottom and get the pieces of your life in order, one by one, so that you can concentrate your efforts on self-actualization, the apex of your potential.

PART III

Your
Climb

CLIMB YOUR
OWN MOUNTAINS

My Son, Oaklan

It felt like he had been enclosed in a glass coffin as he lay there nearly motionless in front of us, his eyes closed and his tiny chest quivering every time he tried to take a breath. His heart was still beating, but his oxygen saturation was declining and his overall chances of survival deteriorating as the hours passed. There were sensors and monitoring wires running to various parts of his body and a thick tube supplying oxygen to a mask covering his entire face. Even with all the medications he had been given, his fever was raging to the point where the critical care nurses had him lying on bags of ice with an ice bag on top of him as well to try to control his body temperature.

The previous few weeks had been a whirlwind of emotions that Natalie and I were experiencing and only beginning to work through. Our second child had been born, a baby boy whom we named Oaklan, and we were settling into our new routine. The doctors were concerned about some of his features after birth, but the majority of indicators were normal, so they took blood samples for genetic testing and discharged us from the regional hospital. It wasn't until almost two weeks after he was born that we received a call from our family doctor confirming that the blood samples had been analyzed and our son had been diagnosed with Down syndrome.

There were a lot of tears shed as we adjusted to the news and to the different trajectory our lives were now on. We wanted the best for all of our children, and the hardest part was embracing the reality of all the additional challenges he would have to face throughout life. The breadth of anticipated physical, mental, emotional, and social difficulties was a lot to take in.

Down syndrome children are particularly susceptible to the respiratory syncytial virus (RSV) that commonly circulates during the winter months, so there is a prophylactic drug course that is normally prescribed to mitigate the potentially life-threatening risk associated with infection. Unfortunately, with the delay in diagnosis and testing for Oaklan, this shot had not been administered, and Oaklan caught RSV.

After a night in our regional hospital, where he twice stopped breathing, he was rushed by ambulance to SickKids hospital in downtown Toronto and, as his situation continued to get worse, to their intensive care unit. Further testing revealed that he also had three holes in his heart along with other complications.

After three agonizing days in intensive care, Oaklan's temperature and respiratory function slowly began to return towards normal, and after ten days, they discharged him from the hospital. He was going to live. And he has lived. He faced his first major challenge and survived.

Without going into all the details of Oaklan's life, it is fair to say that he and our family have had various unique challenges and will continue to encounter more in the years to come. In the midst of these challenges, Natalie and I have often deliberated on what the best next steps are for Oaklan and our family. The approach we have taken has been very much in alignment with the strategies I have been sharing throughout this book. We have embraced each challenge and endeavored to make the most of each situation.

Oaklan has brought us just as much joy and excitement as our two daughters have, and it has been great to watch him develop, learn, and adapt, to keep up with all the activities and adventures our family is involved in. He has been a delightful reminder that fulfillment and meaning in life come from how we approach, work through, and respond to challenges, not from the absence of challenges.

Your Climb

Just as Oaklan is a unique individual with his own challenges and opportunities, you, too, are a unique individual. You have no shortage of your own challenges, obstacles, and misfortunes to contend with in life, and you have no shortage of opportunities within such challenges. Sometimes your opportunities may seem fleeting and your challenges may seem insurmountable, but there is always a way to prevail and make circumstances better.

Your challenges are unique because nobody else on Earth has the exact same personality, heritage, or upbringing that you do, so nobody faces your challenges from your vantage point. In the same way that getting fired from a job can be devastating to one person yet liberating for another, challenges are defined by your perspective. There's little to be gained from comparing your challenges to the challenges others are experiencing; you will never have the whole picture.

Make sure the challenges you seek out are unique to you as well: meaningful endeavors that are important to you, not mountains you're climbing because someone else thinks you should.

The key to safe and successful mountaineering is allowing your body to adapt to new environmental conditions. This is what the acclimatization process is all about, and it is a crucial aspect for mountaineers to respect and appreciate. Failure to adequately adapt in mountaineering is damaging and sometimes fatal. You have to adapt when it comes to inner mountains as well. If you become too rigid in your mindset or approach, you won't be able to adapt mentally and emotionally as your experiences evolve and as you see what is really making a difference in your life.

While a large part of what I've been sharing has focused on individual strategies and looking inward at your own strengths and capacities, the goal is not to isolate yourself from external assistance. It is to aim at getting to the point where you can benefit from the wisdom and support of others without needing to be dependent on them.

In mountaineering, I have seen climbers set out with the mentality that if they get into trouble, there are other climbers and rescue teams that will save them. Their reliance on these external safety nets results in them abdicating their responsibility for planning, training, and preparing for adverse events. When they do inevitably get into trouble, they are fully dependent on others, and if the resources they depend on are unreliable or unavailable when needed, these climbers will often perish.

It is better to be the type of mountaineer who capitalizes on the available knowledge and resources but who ultimately has done the required planning, training, and preparation so that when trouble arises you are competent and capable enough to work through problems and survive, even when your external safety net fails you. This doesn't mean you should avoid external resources and assistance; when resources are available, reach out as needed. But plan your route through life so that you will be ready for challenges.

As you make headway in your own journey, don't forget to celebrate your progress. Don't worry so much about how quickly or effectively those around you seem to be climbing their mountains. What is import is that you are moving forward, and when you look back at where you were yesterday or a week ago, you are in a better place. This is the true measure of whether what you were doing is working for you, regardless of how it is perceived by others or in relation to others. Celebrating every incremental step will also vitalize your momentum and your resolve to continue improving.

Start Climbing Now

We have explored a lot of different challenges and ideas throughout this book, and for each one of them there are countless ways that we could have dived deeper. Such is the nature of the human mind and the near-infinite complexity of life as we know it. Trying to gain a better understanding is often overwhelming and frustrating at the same time, which is why I recommend starting small and building from there.

I hope you have found some of what I have learned on my journey to be beneficial to you. Remember to implement that which you determine to be helpful and disregard that which you don't. As I said at the beginning, my aim with this book is not to deliver expedient miracles, it is to show you additional tools to keep in your toolbox for success: another weapon in your arsenal or an ice axe in your mountaineering pack for when you inevitably encounter adversity in life.

If our paths have not yet crossed in person, I hope that we do have a chance to meet someday, and I wish you success in your own journey. Identify the summits that you need to work on the most and persist in your commitment to continual improvement. My sincere hope is that the examples and strategies that I have shared with you throughout this book will be a catalyst in propelling you to take a step forward, and then another step. You have the potential within you to scale whatever mountains life throws at you and those mountains you actively seek out as well.

I'll end by paraphrasing an old proverb, originally about the best time to plant a tree: If we want to reach the summits in our own lives, the best time to have started climbing was when we were children. The second-best time would have been throughout our adolescent years. But we can't change the past; we can only look forward from where we are today and do our best to plan and take the right route into our future. So the very best time available to start climbing is right now, in this moment. Make the commitment, take the action, and make the future you deserve a reality.

ABOUT THE AUTHOR

 ALAN MALLORY is an international speaker, author, and performance coach who is passionate about personal growth and reaching new heights in all that we do. His unique philosophy of life revolves around empowering people and embracing an agile mentality focused on relationships and results.

Alan holds a degree in engineering from Queen's University and a master's in psychology from Adler University, giving him a well-balanced approach to the outer and inner challenges we face. Before embarking on his current vocation in speaking and training, he worked all over the world as a professional engineer and project manager, developing patents and solutions to complex challenges in the mining and metals sector.

Building experience through a lifestyle of adventure and challenge, Alan embarked on the journey of a lifetime and set a world record on Mount Everest along with three members of his immediate family. It was a two-month expedition through some of the most exciting yet terrifying conditions imaginable.

Although Alan continues to pursue many athletic and adventurous endeavors, his deeper focus is on the mountains within each of us: moving beyond the mental and emotional challenges that hold us back and becoming the best that we can be. Climbing his own internal Everest—a journey of personal growth through anxiety and depression—fueled Alan's passion for discovering and articulating strategies that improve people's lives. It is this work that Alan finds most fulfilling.